SpringerBriefs in Computer Science

More information about this series at http://www.springer.com/series/10028

Rae Earnshaw

Research and Development in the Academy, Creative Industries and Applications

Springer

Rae Earnshaw
Centre for Visual Computing,
Faculty of Engineering and Informatics
University of Bradford
Bradford
UK

and

School of Creative Arts
Wrexham Glyndŵr University
Wrexham
UK

ISSN 2191-5768 ISSN 2191-5776 (electronic)
SpringerBriefs in Computer Science
ISBN 978-3-319-54080-1 ISBN 978-3-319-54081-8 (eBook)
DOI 10.1007/978-3-319-54081-8

Library of Congress Control Number: 2017932785

Printed on acid-free paper

This Springer imprint is published by Springer Nature
The registered company is Springer International Publishing AG
The registered company address is: Gewerbestrasse 11, 6330 Cham, Switzerland

Foreword

Evolution is hard, and sometimes harsh; clearly that is often the case as universities evolve to expand their missions and compete for funds and students and grants and, increasingly, for opportunities to collaborate with industry. In this book, Rae Earnshaw helps us understand the changing ecosystem within which today's universities must operate, and to which they must adapt their internal structures and perhaps even governance forms. He notes that the role of modern university is evolving, and doing so seemingly more rapidly in recent decades; it is becoming increasingly relevant to aspects of national economic growth. This growth, along with the increasing economic relevance of the creative industries, is introduced and outlined in this book, a successor to his "Research and Development in Art Design and Creativity," which examined how communication, collaboration, and creativity can facilitate *the development of applications* including especially those related to art, design, and creative industries.

Rae Earnshaw, whom I first met well over a decade ago on the IEEE Computer Graphics and Applications Magazine Editorial Board, is superbly qualified to write this book on university–industry collaboration and R&D in creative industries and applications. He not only has a solid research background but also has held leadership roles from Head of Department to Pro Vice Chancellor, and been involved in large joint university–industry projects.

The collaboration models and issues Rae correctly identifies are significant and important. I have worked in both industrial and academic worlds, having begun at the General Motors Research Labs, later moving to Simon Fraser University. I have experienced the benefits and frustrations—on both sides—that Rae describes. And within academia, I have been on both sides of the computer science—creative arts divide, having spent over a decade in each, and been involved in large university-industry collaborative projects.

This book gives a concise view not only of the current state, but also the current change vector of academia's role vis-a-vis industry, especially with respect to creative industry.

Each chapter has a valuable set of 'lessons learned' which help illustrate and support major points. Additionally, a set of three case studies provide supporting evidence for the lessons.

It is helpful to remember the book's objective is to provide a summary of the main points—what is established, what is currently being researched and developed; and what are the expected ongoing issues and options for the future. Thus it is more an executive briefing—an update of current issues in the field. It is not intended to include every aspect in the fields being addressed. Those wanting more detail can find it by exploring the extensive 'further reading' lists and the references.

I believe this book will be of interest to Vice-Presidents of Research, whether in academia or industry. It is a very compact overview of R&D in the creative industries, with an appropriately broad definition of creative, and with a focus on collaboration between industry and academia. It is also appropriate for department heads and R&D project leaders in industry and academia and for government policy-makers.

Vancouver, Canada
January 2017

John C. Dill

Preface

The first book[1] in this subject area covered the key aspects of collaboration and communication in Research and Development (R&D), and how technology may be used to support creativity in the R&D process. This included how research and development in art and design may be formulated, and framed, and then evaluated and measured, and the valuable contribution that art and design makes to the scientific and technological enterprise and vice-versa.

This book brings together an analysis of the current methodologies for research and development in the academy and industry with a number of illustrative Case Studies. The latter are used to review how the processes of research, development, and implementation work out in practice.

Creative industries are increasingly being seen as important local and national components of revenue generation and job creation, as well as potential catalysts on the wider front of social inclusion, cultural diversity, and human development. This book also recognizes the challenges that interdisciplinary working on content creation can bring and provides suggestions in Chap. 3 on how to address these.

The academy and industry are each currently facing a number of significant challenges. The academy faces funding cuts, an increasing proportion of part-time and adjunct faculty, and increasing competition from commercial providers. Industry faces the challenge of a global market, the rise of Asia, and periodic economic downturn.

The tensions and different ways of working between the academy and industry are well summarized in Chap. 2. Whilst these technical and cultural issues can still present ongoing difficulties, they are resolvable by mutual understanding and support between the partners, and a common and united desire to achieve agreed objectives and outcomes.

In Chaps. 2 and 4, the book details the various ways in which the academy and industry can collaborate. Therefore irrespective of the current position of the

---

[1]Earnshaw, R.A.: Research and Development in Art, Design and Creativity. Springer (2016) http://dx.doi.org/10.1007/978-3-319-33005-1.

academy in the spectrum of options, there is normally scope for a collaboration to be established. The current trend in agency-funded research and development is towards larger collaborations in order to be able to effectively address significant societal and industrial problems and challenges. This represents a major opportunity for the academy to demonstrate the innovation and creativity that has characterized its activity in the past, and which continues into the present.

New ideas and new discoveries are key to the future. Entrepreneurial expertise is needed to migrate these ideas into practical applications and value-added products and services. Chapter 4 discusses the parameters of the academy–industry collaboration and how success can be achieved.

This book examines how creativity can characterize and support research and development from an idea to an industrial product or service in typical creative application areas and technology deliverables. Collaboration between the academy and the industry is examined and the factors leading to successful products and services are identified. The process of initial idea through to design and successful implementation is a pipeline. Creative applications are increasingly becoming dependent on information technology and there is a need to understand how this may be optimized in terms of utilization resources and also ease of interfacing to the user. A number of factors tend to be generic and permeate many application areas (such as device handling, bandwidth requirements, use of color, interaction methods) while others are more customized with specialist hardware and software (e.g., shared virtual environments, augmented reality), though the latter are increasingly being run on the Internet with low-cost devices and are aimed at a mass market (e.g., Pokémon Go). This trend is likely to continue since the objective is to be able to utilize commodity products and thereby increase market penetration.

This book has selected three Case Studies and examines how they are implemented and what lessons can be learned from the successes or failures in aspects of the implementation. Two of these Case Studies are in creative applications; the third is on a wider industrial project. Thus Chaps. 1–4 detail the aspects associated with research and development and the collaboration between the academy and industry. Three chapters detail the Case Studies and have been authored and contributed by those involved directly in the work in these areas. Each Case Study contains a section on the lessons learned from the project. Many of these lessons are generic in nature and should be useful to readers developing their own applications. The first two Case Studies are primarily in the creative industry areas. The third Case Study is in the physical sciences area and is therefore more classical in its approach and involves a university and an industrial company with cognate interests in a scientific area of the academy. However, the lessons learned are also primarily generic in nature and should be useful to those involved in the creative industries areas.

Each Case Study is authored by a specialist author (or authors) and they are detailed in the Acknowledgements section at the end of this Preface.

Creative industries are estimated to be making an increasing contribution to a nation's economy through wealth and job creation. The basic resources are ideas and information which are transformed into cultural goods and services through a group of linked activities. Application areas currently include advertising, publishing, design, digital media, computer games, museums, galleries, music, and visual arts. Digital platforms enable the user to access content and services. Digital convergence is bringing together information technology, telecommunications, and media. The market for creative industries is global and competitive. Thus content and services need to meet a user need, be attractive, and be easy to access and use. This requires creativity, skill, talent, and innovation often across a number of sectors during the research and development processes.

The creative industries face a unique mixture of both challenges and opportunities because of their mixture of disciplines and varied backgrounds of the practitioners and researchers. Working within their own particular disciplines, researchers will typically find it comfortable and familiar to develop and evaluate ideas and processes utilizing the methodologies that are traditionally associated with, or are intrinsic to, their discipline. The challenges and opportunities occur where cross- and interdisciplinary works take place. This leads to two issues relating to research: first, how to effectively support and nurture cross- and interdisciplinary research in the creative industries and second, how to ensure that where crossdisciplinary work takes place, then it adds value to the product or service being developed.

The University of Bradford, UK, pioneered the area of digital media in the mid-1990s by tripartite collaborations between technology, art and design, and media and broadcasting. It was done by setting up a new academic department because it did not sit easily within existing academic disciplines and structures. It was very successful in attracting students and also meeting the needs and requirements of industry. It also highlighted the benefits and advantages of interdisciplinary collaborations. Involvement in a number of large interdisciplinary European Projects over the years at the Universities of Leeds and Bradford required research and development in a number of application areas, such as multimedia assets for design, collaborative visualization over networks, and virtual entertainment, and led to a number of important results. These are detailed in the first book referred to above.

Involvement as a professor in the School Creative Arts at Glyndwr University, Wales, over recent years has provided opportunity to think about these aspects, and publish a number of papers in collaboration with the faculty.

It is hoped that this book makes a useful contribution to an important area of discussion and debate.

Acknowledgements

Chapters 5, 6, and 7 are Case Studies and thanks are expressed to all the authors who contributed these chapters. Chapter 5 "*Shared Virtual and Augmented Environments for Creative Applications*" was supplied by Prof. Alexei Sourin, Nanyang Technological University, Singapore. Chapter 6 "*Digital Holography as a*

Creative Medium to Display and Re-interpret Museum Artefacts, Applied to Chinese Porcelain Masterpieces" was supplied by Dr. Shuo Wang, Dr. Ardeshir Osanlou and Prof. Peter S. Excell, Wrexham Glyndwr University, UK. Chapter 7 "*Improving the Physical Properties of Materials by Collaboration between Industry and the Academy*" was supplied by Dr. Elvin Nix, UK.

Thanks and appreciation are due to all those who read draft versions of the chapters and provided comments to improve technical content and readability. However, responsibility for the final text rests with the author.

Thanks are expressed to colleagues and students at the School of Creative Arts at Wrexham Glyndwr University, Wales, for many useful discussions.

Thanks are expressed to John Dill for providing the Foreword to the book.

Thanks and appreciation are also due to Springer for assistance and support with the production of the book and e-book.

Bradford, UK
January 2017

Rae Earnshaw

Contents

Chapter 1
History and Background: The Development of the Academy and Industry

Abstract Historically, higher education institutions have been engaged in teaching and research and organized and run by their communities of scholars. The first universities in Europe which were founded in the eleventh and twelfth centuries mainly followed an Aristotelian and Greek model of understanding of the world, and concentrated on abstract subjects such as logic and grammar. The widening of knowledge about the natural world achieved through the Renaissance, the Scientific Revolution, and the Industrial Revolution from the fourteenth to the nineteenth centuries resulted in a transition from the medieval university to more modern forms which included a wider range of disciplines, particularly in the areas of science and technology. Generally, universities grant degrees at undergraduate and postgraduate levels and so have defined curricula and assessment criteria for these standards of learning. Some institutions are more applied (e.g., The German Technical Universities) and established an early priority for also providing students with the skills and expertise which were of direct relevance to industry. Historically, it was accepted that faculty have academic freedom which allowed them to educate and research in discipline areas of their choice, but the rapid expansion of knowledge and the time required to master an area in depth has resulted in increasing degrees of specialization by faculty. This in turn has increased their potential value in advancing the state of the art in both research and in industry. Thus the growth and expansion of the academy has resulted in an increasing awareness on the part of governments and industry of the economic value of research and development, and the potential contribution that the academy can make to industry and wider society.

Keywords Applied research · Bayh–Dole act · Technology transfer · Knowledge exchange · Globalization · Technology transfer offices · Small- and medium-sized enterprises

R. Earnshaw, *Research and Development in the Academy, Creative Industries and Applications*, SpringerBriefs in Computer Science,
DOI 10.1007/978-3-319-54081-8_1

1.1 Introduction

Early European higher education dates back to the sixth century and was the province of cathedral and monastic schools where monks and nuns gave lectures. The earliest universities in Europe with a formal structure were Bologna, Paris, and Oxford in the eleventh and twelfth centuries. European universities expanded rapidly rom the fifteenth to nineteenth centuries. Initially they continued the approach taken during the Middle Ages and subjects studied included natural philosophy, logic, theology, mathematics, astronomy (and astrology), law, grammar, rhetoric, and medicine. This was therefore essentially a generalist approach.

The scientific revolution (1550–1700) and the subsequent industrial revolution (1760–1840) and their requirements for scientific analysis, resulted in a more specialist scholar proficient in these new methods and approaches. Thus university training was essential in order to be able to perform scientific analysis to the accepted standards and also to have assurance that the results of the work would be examined by the scientific community.

Prior emphasis upon theology in universities decreased during the nineteenth century and the new model of higher learning evidenced by institutions in Germany and France was followed by many countries, including the USA, where Johns Hopkins University was one of the first to follow the German research university model. The rise of the modern university also increased access to students.

The German technical university (originally termed Technische Hochschule) concentrated on engineering disciplines. Initially there appeared to be a view that they should not be regarded as universities because of their concentration on applied subjects, but the granting of their right to award the doctoral degree soon resulted in a recognition of their parity with other universities (and some changed their name formally to Technical University to remove any ambiguity). The German technical university was an early indication of the priority in Germany for producing graduates with both academic knowledge and appropriate and effective skills to assist industry.

In the UK the Robbins Report in 1963 stated that higher education institutions should have the following objectives [1, 2]:

- instruction in skills
- the promotion of the general powers of the mind so as to produce not mere specialists but rather cultivated men and women
- to maintain research in balance with teaching, since teaching should not be separated from the advancement of learning and the search for truth
- to transmit a common culture and common standards of citizenship.

The Dearing Report in 1997 set out a vision for the longer term future of higher education in the UK. It was more concerned with expanding student numbers and did not specifically address the potential for the academy to contribute to industry. However, it did recognize the importance of the following [3]:

- higher education's contribution to basic, strategic, and applied research should be maintained and enhanced, particularly in subjects where UK research has attained international standards of excellence or in Technology Foresight priority areas.

Over time the number of universities in the UK has steadily increased. Under the Further and Higher Education Act 1992, the former polytechnics became universities and awarded their own degrees. Their former emphasis on training for trade skills was largely replaced by traditional degrees. Participation in higher education in the UK has risen from around 5% of in the 1960s to around 50% today.

It has been argued [4] that for the period 1870–1970, the USA was less dependent on research and development from the academy because key developments such as the harnessing of electricity and the development of the internal combustion engine developed more through inventor-entrepreneurs in the wider society. They facilitated a growth in productivity in the USA as a whole. However, it is clear that today's high technology developments tend to require more specialized, high-cost, equipment, and advanced research which are the natural province of the academy. It has also been argued [5] that profit-making businesses have better ideas and better expertise than the academy for developing better products which are fully market tested. However, it is recognized that the academy produces graduates with the abilities and skills who are able to accomplish such developments in industry. This intellectual capital is in itself is a form of technology transfer from the academy to industry.

1.2 The Bayh–Dole Act

> Before the passing of the Bayh-Dole Act in 1980, the ownership of any intellectual property generated by research funded by the US government was undefined. The Act, which passed into US legislation, resulted in all US Universities, small businesses and nonprofit organisations being able to utilize the intellectual property arising from such funding. It was a recognition of two factors. Firstly, before the Bayh-Dole Act the US government had accumulated 30,000 patents of which only 5% had been licensed commercially. Clearly this was a significant waste of assets and there was much greater scope for direct commercialization if those involved with generating the patents could also exploit them. Secondly, after World War II it was clear that there was significant potential in US Universities to contribute directly to the rapidly developing fields of science, engineering, medicine, and health [6].

The effects of the Bayh–Dole Act in its early years on US research and technology transfer are summarized by Mowery et al. [7, 8] and Earnshaw [9].

1.3 Silicon Valley, USA

In the southern San Francisco Bay Area of California, Silicon Valley is home to many start-ups and global technology companies along with associated support companies, such as those supplying venture capital and other services. Apple, Facebook, and Google are among the most well known. Stanford University is also the site of technology-focused institutions centered around Palo Alto and has a long history of providing technology and expertise for high-technology start-up companies. It accounts for one-third of all of the venture capital investment in the USA. Silicon Valley was associated with the silicon-based integrated circuit, the microprocessor, and the microcomputer, among other key technologies. The region employs about one-quarter of a million information technology workers.

> Perhaps the strongest thread that runs through the Valley's past and present is the drive to 'play' with novel technology, which, when bolstered by an advanced engineering degree and channeled by astute management, has done much to create the industrial powerhouse we see in the Valley today [10, 11].

Scaruffi [12] provides a history of Silicon Valley.

1.4 Fraunhofer, Germany

Technology Transfer in Germany—the Fraunhofer Model

Applied research is one of the foundation principles of the Fraunhofer organization, which is one of the leading organizations for applied research in Europe. It partners with companies to transform original ideas into innovations that benefit society and strengthen both the German and the European economy. Its research activities are conducted by 67 institutes and research units at locations throughout Germany. Affiliated international research centers and representative offices provide contact with the regions of greatest importance to present and future scientific progress and economic development [13].

> The Fraunhofer Institutes receive 20-30% of their total income from the government based on the degree to which they generate contract work for public and commercial clients. Thus the agenda is primarily demand-driven. However, the classic research ethos is maintained by appointing directors of Fraunhofer Institutes who are also professors with research programs within their Universities. Thus the Fraunhofer establishes a direct bridge between the academy and industry. It is also particularly relevant for European multi-partner research grants where a combination of academic and industrial expertise is often required in the consortium. The Fraunhofer gives priority to work directed to the areas of health, security, communication, energy and the environment. As a result, the work undertaken by researchers and developers can have a significant impact on people's lives. The advantage of the institutes being organized into one overall framework provides opportunity for the development of an overall national strategy which is coherent and ensures added-value across the network. In addition, it can provide access by all the institutes to specialist centres of expertise or high cost equipment (e.g., for nanotechnology) [14].

The accumulation of fundamental research led to the establishment of an institute in the areas of computer graphics, visualization, and virtual reality at the University of Darmstadt [15, 16].

1.5 Historical Developments in the UK on Collaboration Between the Academy and Industry

This section utilizes the UK as a case study to highlight the ways in which the UK has sought to strengthen the links between the academy and industry and also to provide assistance and support where further development was deemed to be appropriate.

1.5.1 Alvey Programme for Research and Development in Information Technology

The Alvey Programme in the UK was an initiative to develop applied Information Technology research in the period 1983–1988 [17]. One driver for this was the perceived challenge raised by Japan's Fifth Generation Computer Programme in late 1981. Prior to the Alvey Programme, university, industrial and government research were primarily separate activities. The Science and Engineering Research Council evaluated research proposals from the academy by peer-review. In the late 1970s, the former Science and Engineering Research Council (SERC) had become more proactive with the appearance of calls for specific areas that were regarded as of special importance or priority. This provided for coordinated programmes in particular areas.

The Alvey Programme made a change to the way applied computing research was organized in the UK as a whole. For a variety of reasons, it was decided that there needed to be a more focused way of doing industrial and university research in this important area.

Some of the main points were:

- The area was *pre-competitive* advanced information technology research
- The focus was four areas that seemed particularly relevant at the time:
  - Software Engineering
  - Intelligent Knowledge Based Systems
  - Man Machine Interaction
  - Advanced Microelectronics (VLSI Design)
- Research was a *collaboration* between academia, government, and industry
- Research was *directed* into important areas and *coordinated*
- Funding was *substantial*, £350 M at 1982 prices.

Alvey Report

> This report explores how Britain can maintain its competitive advantage in the challenging new area of Information Technology (IT). The launching of Japan's Fifth Generation Computer Programme in late 1981 could well mark a new epoch in IT. The Programme aims to apply IT in areas where existing systems have proved inadequate and to produce substantial increases in efficiency and productivity in information-dependent industries. The Programme will develop IT for knowledge processing as opposed to the current fields of data processing and computation.
>
> The report recommends a five-year programme to mobilise the UK's technical strengths in IT, through a Government-backed collaborative effort between industry, the academic sector and other research organisations. The goal is a strong UK capability in the *core* enabling technologies, essential to Britain's future competitiveness in the world IT market [18].

1.5.2 Lambert Review of Industrial Collaboration

In the UK in 2003, the Lambert Review [19] was initiated to address the following three objectives:

- To recognize the changing nature of industrial R&D such as outsourcing, and the increasingly global nature of R&D due to the Internet and international competition
- To benefit from successful role models of collaboration between the academy and industry that had already benefited the UK economy
- To make recommendations for the future.

The review recognized that research in the academy operated on international networks, particularly that in the internationally leading institutions. There was potential therefore for industry to benefit by linking in with these. The review noted that a key performance indicator was the total spend of the UK on R&D as a percentage of the Gross Domestic Product (GDP). When compared with leading nations such as the USA and Germany it was noted to be lower and needed to be increased. The review supported the UK government's third-stream funding (i.e., in addition to teaching and research) established in 2001 and proposed that this be expanded. This Higher Education Innovation Fund (HEIF) provides funding direct to institutions to support business/academy collaborations.

The Government Treasury advised that [20]:

> *the best form of knowledge transfer comes when a talented researcher moves out of the university and into business, or vice versa [p12].*
>
> *the most exciting collaborations arise as a result of like-minded people getting together—sometimes by chance—to address a problem [p12].*
>
> *encouraging academics and business people to spend more time together should be a high priority for knowledge transfer professionals [p12].*

the innovation process is nonlinear, so knowledge transfer is not simply a question of channeling clever ideas from researchers down a production line into commercialisation. "Great ideas emerge out of all kinds of feedback loops, development activities and sheer chance. This is another reason why it is so critical to build dynamic networks between academic researchers and their business counterparts" [p12].

diversity is good, both in mission and in funding. "The type of business collaboration that would make sense for one kind of university might be either impossible or irrelevant for another" [p13].

proximity matters when it comes to business collaboration [p13].

"business-university collaborations need careful and consistent management by both sides, and a number of joint programmes have failed for lack of such attention" [p13].

an emphasis on knowledge transfer requires institutions to put in place new mechanisms for establishing institutional priorities [p13].

universities are more complex to manage than businesses, with a variety of different stakeholders—academics, students, and funders [p13].

that the large number of pots of ring-fenced financing is 'the source of endless unnecessary frustration' [p13].

1.5.3 Further Reviews of Academy–Industry Collaborations in the UK

There have been further government reviews of academy–industry collaborations in the UK since Alvey and Lambert. These are documented online [21–29].

1.6 Dual Funding in the UK

The UK operates a dual funding system for research [30]. Firstly, an amount is distributed to each institution determined by a periodic (usually every 5 years) national and international audit of research quality in each discipline in each institution (the Research Assessment). This amount is known as the Quality Related (QR) funding stream and remains constant for the next 5 years to provide a secure and stable baseline for funding research, and is supplied to institutions on an annual basis. The Higher Education Funding Council for England distributes approximately £1.6 billion in 2016–17 via this mechanism [31]. The second aspect is the funding of grant proposals submitted to the national research councils. Total annual funding is approximately £3 billion (to cover all the areas of science, engineering, biosciences, medical, economics and social science, arts and humanities) by peer review of grant bids [32].

1.7 Knowledge Exchange in the UK

Knowledge Exchange Funding (Higher Education Innovation Funding in the UK) for 2016–17 is approximately £160 million and provides direct funding to support the development of academy/industry collaborations [33]. This can also be used to support and strengthen central Technology Transfer Offices in institutions.

Knowledge Transfer Partnerships (KTP) foster innovation in a business by linking it with a university and a recently qualified graduate who works at the company, and who brings new skills and knowledge to the business. A KTP can last 12–36 months depending on the project and the requirements of the business [34].

Collaboration between the academy and industrial is particularly relevant to Small and Medium-sized Enterprises (SME). They are estimated to represent 99% of all businesses in the European Union [35]. They are often responsible for driving innovation and therefore can benefit from access to leading edge developments in the academy.

1.8 Apprenticeships in the UK

Apprenticeships offer students the opportunity to both work in a company and study part-time to degree level [36, 37]. They can also ensure continuation of employment on graduation.

1.9 Lessons Learned

The development of the academy from the Middle Ages to today has demonstrated some interesting features. Initially concentrating on abstract and theoretical disciplines it has widened over time to include science and technology—largely brought about the developments in the Scientific and Industrial Revolutions. Universities also developed regular audits and reviews—in order to compare with curriculum developments and best practice in research and development in other international universities. Where such universities had successful collaborations with industry, these were noted.

1.10 Conclusions

The history of the development of the academy and its collaboration with industry has been reviewed. Developments in the USA, Germany, and the UK have been highlighted. The potential for the future is set out in Chap. 2.

Further Reading

Anderson, R.: The idea of a university' today. United Kingdom: Hist. Policy. http://www.historyandpolicy.org/policy-papers/papers/the-idea-of-a-university-today (2010)

Clark, B.R.: Creating Entrepreneurial Universities: Organizational Pathways of Transformation, p. 180. Pergamon, Oxford (1998)

Collini, S.: What are Universities For?, p. 240. Penguin, London (2012)

Headrick, D.R.: The Tentacles of Progress: Technology Transfer in the Age of Imperialism, 1850–1940, p. 420. Oxford University Press, Oxford (1990)

Newman, J. H.: The Idea of a University. p. 354, Aeterna Press, London (2015). ISBN-10: 1785165313 (originally published 1852). http://www.newmanreader.org/works/idea/

Oakley, B.: Alvey: Britain's Strategic Computing Initiative, p. 354. MIT Press, Boston, MA (1990). ISBN-10: 0262150387, ISBN-13: 978-0262150385

https://www.amazon.co.uk/Alvey-Britains-Strategic-Computing-Initiative/dp/0262150387/ref=sr_1_1?s=books&ie=UTF8&qid=1472818144&sr=1-1&keywords=Alvey%3A+Britain%27s+Strategic +Computing+Initiative

Rosegrant, S., Lampe, D.: Route 128: Lessons from Boston's High-Tech Community (Reprint edition), p. 256. Basic Books, New York (1993)

Scaruffi, P.: A History of Silicon Valley: Almost a 3rd Edition—2015. CreateSpace Independent Publishing Platform, p. 504 (2015)

Technology Transfer Systems in the United States and Germany: Lessons and Perspectives. Fraunhofer Institute for Systems and Innovation Research, National Academy of Engineering, Binational Panel Convened by The National Academy of Engineering and The Fraunhofer Society, p. 448, National Academies Press, Washington DC (1997)

What are Universities for? http://www.universityworldnews.com/article.php?story=20090326200944986

References

1. http://www.educationengland.org.uk/documents/robbins/robbins1963.html
2. https://en.wikipedia.org/wiki/Robbins_Report
3. http://www.educationengland.org.uk/documents/dearing1997/dearing1997.html
4. Gordon, R.J.: The Rise and Fall of American Growth. p. 784. Princeton University Press, Princeton, NJ (2016). ISBN-10: 0691147728
5. McCloskey, D.: The Ultimate Resource, p. 734. Princeton University Press, Princeton, NJ (1998) ISBN-10: 0691003815
6. http://en.wikipedia.org/wiki/Bayh%E2%80%93Dole_Act
7. Mowery, D.C., Nelson, R.R., Sampat, B.N., Ziedonis, A.A.: The Effects of the Bayh-Dole Act on U.S. University Research and Technology Transfer. In: Branscomb, L., Kodama, F., Florida, R. (eds.) Industrializing Knowledge, pp. 269–306, MIT Press, Cambridge, MA (1999)
8. Mowery, D.C., Nelson, R.R.: Ivory Tower and Industrial Innovation: University-Industry Technology before and after the Bayh-Dole Act (Stanford Business Books). Stanford University Press, Stanford, CA (2004)
9. Earnshaw, R.A.: Knowledge Exchange, Technology Transfer and the Academy. In: Dill, J., Earnshaw, R.A., Kasik, D.J., Wong, P.C. (eds.) Expanding the Frontiers of Visual Analytics and Visualization, pp. 469–480. Springer, London (2012). ISBN: 978-1-4471-2803-9. http://link.springer.com/chapter/10.1007%2F978-1-4471-2804-5_26

10. Sturgeon, T. J.: How Silicon Valley Came to Be. In: Kenney, M. (ed.) Understanding Silicon Valley: The Anatomy of an Entrepreneurial Region. Stanford University, Stanford, CA. ISBN 978-0-8047-3734-0. https://en.wikipedia.org/wiki/Silicon_Valley (2000). Retrieved 24 Mar 2015
11. https://en.wikipedia.org/wiki/Silicon_Valley
12. Scaruffi, P.: A History of Silicon Valley: Almost a 3rd Edition—2015, p. 504. CreateSpace Independent Publishing Platform (2015)
13. https://www.fraunhofer.de/en/institutes.html
14. http://www.fraunhofer.de/en/about-fraunhofer/http://www.fraunhofer.de/en/institutes-research-establishments/
15. Earnshaw, R.A.: Fraunhofer Institute—Building on a Decade of Computer Graphics Research. IEEE Comput. Graphics Appl. **18**(2), 10–16 (1998). doi:10.1109/38.656784
16. http://ieeexplore.ieee.org/xpl/freeabs_all.jsp?arnumber=656784 http://www.igd.fraunhofer.de/
17. http://www.chilton-computing.org.uk/inf/alvey/overview.htm
18. http://www.chilton-computing.org.uk/inf/literature/reports/alvey_report/overview.htm
19. Lambert, R.,: Lambert Review of Business University Collaboration, p. 142. http://www.eua.be/eua/jsp/en/upload/lambert_review_final_450.1151581102387.pdf http://www.hm-treasury.gov.uk/d/lambertemergingissues_173.pdf (2003)
20. http://en.wikipedia.org/wiki/Lambert_Review
21. The Dowling Review of Business-University Collaborations. http://www.raeng.org.uk/policy/dowling-review/the-dowling-review-of-business-university-research (2015)
22. Making industry-university partnerships work—Lessons from successful collaborations, p. 52. http://www.sciencebusiness.net/Assets/94fe6d15-5432-4cf9-a656-633248e63541.pdf http://www.sciencebusiness.net/ourReports/reportDetail.aspx?ReportId=33
23. UK Research and the EU, The Royal Society. https://royalsociety.org/news/2015/12/UK%20research%20and%20EU/ (2015)
24. Wilson, T.: A Review of Business-University Collaboration, p. 89. https://www.gov.uk/government/uploads/system/uploads/attachment_data/file/32383/12-610-wilson-review-business-university-collaboration.pdf http://dera.ioe.ac.uk/13842/1/wilson.pdf https://www.gov.uk/government/news/give-universities-bigger-role-in-growing-economy-witty (2012)
25. UK House of Commons—Business University Collaboration 2014–15, p. 42. http://www.publications.parliament.uk/pa/cm201415/cmselect/cmbis/249/249.pdf (2015)
26. Universities, Business and Knowledge Exchange—University of Cambridge, p. 64. http://www.cbr.cam.ac.uk/fileadmin/user_upload/centre-for-business-research/downloads/special-reports/specialreport-universitiesbusinessknowledgeexchange.pdf (2008)
27. CBI—Best of Both Worlds—Guide to Business-University Collaboration, p. 40 http://www.cbi.org.uk/cbi-prod/assets/File/pdf/Best_of_both_worlds.pdf
28. Creative Industries Strategy, p. 31. http://www.thecreativeindustries.co.uk/media/243587/cic_report_final-hi-res-.pdf (2012)
29. Encouraging a British Invention Revolution: Sir Andrew Witty's Review of Universities and Growth, p. 147 https://www.gov.uk/government/uploads/system/uploads/attachment_data/file/249720/bis-13-1241-encouraging-a-british-invention-revolution-andrew-witty-review-R1.pdf (2013)
30. http://www.hefce.ac.uk/rsrch/funding/
31. http://www.hefce.ac.uk/rsrch/funding/mainstream/
32. http://www.rcuk.ac.uk/research/
33. http://www.hefce.ac.uk/pubs/year/2016/201609/
34. http://ktp.innovateuk.org/ https://www.gov.uk/guidance/knowledge-transfer-partnerships-what-they-are-and-how-to-apply
35. http://ec.europa.eu/growth/smes/business-friendly-environment/sme-definition_en https://en.wikipedia.org/wiki/Small_and_medium-sized_enterprises
36. https://www.gov.uk/topic/further-education-skills/apprenticeships
37. http://www.learndirect.com/business/products-and-services/apprenticeships/what-are-the-benefits-of-apprenticeships-to-your-business/

Chapter 2
Models of Interaction Between the Academy and Industry

Abstract Education has been accepted by the leaders of society as an overall public good and able to provide expertize to address difficult problems and produce solutions. Technical universities, or institutes of technology, had by definition a closer relationship to society since they were more concerned with the applied aspects of science and technology, which were of more immediate interest to those in society seeking to solve real-world problems. It is this latter aspect which has resulted in the widening agenda for the academy as a whole—in seeking to understand how it can play an effective role without diminishing its longstanding traditions of excellence in the core areas of teaching and research. In some cases this has been driven by government policy where the government provides some, or all, of the required financial support to the university. In other cases, it has been driven by financial necessity where there is little, or no, government financial support, and the institution has to generate its own income streams to support its mission and its teaching and research programmes. In a competitive market place and the increasing globalization of business, industry increasingly seeks to use strategies, tools and techniques that increase efficiency and effectiveness, whilst at the same time maximizing quality and minimizing cost. Companies may consider outsourcing their Research and Development requirements to reduce corporate overheads and optimize staffing levels. This means that Universities and other private laboratories can utilize the opportunity and look to collaborate with industry to supply this expertize on terms that are mutually acceptable and beneficial. Universities also generate their own spin-outs from intellectual property they create, as well as licensing technology to industry, rather than transferring it. However, the relationship between university and industry is not without its cultural differences and challenges, chief of which is the historical commitment of the academy to advance knowledge whether it is immediately applicable or not. In addition, there are many fundamental and important long-term research issues that many would argue are the primary duty of the academy to address, which may have no direct application in the short to medium term. This is resulting in increasing tensions in the academy, and in the priorities for national and international funding agencies. A variety of models of interaction between the academy and industry have been developed depending on the one hand on the circumstances of the institution, its

R. Earnshaw, *Research and Development in the Academy, Creative Industries and Applications*, SpringerBriefs in Computer Science,
DOI 10.1007/978-3-319-54081-8_2

mission, its values, its expertize and its relationship to the local and cultural environment in which it is situated. On the other hand, there are factors to do with local and national industry including their needs and requirements, their methods of operation, and the degree to which the expertize in the academy may be utilized to advantage. The pros and cons of these various models are reviewed, and lessons learned are summarized.

Keywords Industrial collaboration · Marketization of the academy · Science and technology parks · Innovation · Intellectual property · Non-disclosure agreement · Knowledge-based economy · Knowledge transfer · Economic development · Blue-sky research

2.1 Introduction

National and international funding agencies generally support pure research via open and focussed calls for grant proposals which are evaluated by peer review. These have been an integral part of academy research for many years and are expected to lead to outputs including external publication in peer-reviewed journals and conferences, and patents.

Recent trends in the academy have been characterized by one or more of the following factors:

- Greater participation of students in many countries in higher education (rising from 5% of the population 50 years ago to over 50% today).
- Increasing marketization of higher education to more directly meet the needs of those who wish to utilize its services.
- The trend to top-down management models resulting in corporate universities where power and authority are transferred from faculty to managers and economic justifications dominate.
- An increasing environment of austerity due to national and international downturns in economies.
- The need to generate additional income streams in the academy to address funding shortfalls.
- The widening of the traditional academic role of faculty from research and teaching to also include collaboration with industry (e.g., [1]).

This has resulted in increasing attention being paid in the academy to the opportunities of interacting with industry, and exploring how effective collaboration to the benefit of both parties might be achieved.

Interaction with industry and knowledge transfer has already made considerable advances in many countries [2, 3], particularly those with well-established connections between academia and industry in the generation of world-leading products and services (e.g., Silicon Valley in the USA). As economies advance, it is argued that they migrate from resource-based to knowledge-based production. Thus knowledge and innovation are two of the factors behind job creation and economic growth. This in turn affects the social context and also public and economic policy. Many national governments have therefore sought to address the challenges implicit in this observation and, in particular, provide motivation and incentives to increase the collaboration between industry and the academy in the expectation that there will be direct benefits to a nation's economy and overall global competitiveness. In turn, the academy has sought to address the challenges and opportunities where they align with their institutional mission. Clark [4] used the phrase "*entrepreneurial universities*" to characterize the aspects of promoting technology transfer within national systems of learning and innovation. Whether public or private, industry increasingly seeks to use tools and techniques that increase efficiency and effectiveness, whilst at the same time maximizing quality and minimizing cost. The current trend towards companies outsourcing their Research and Development (R&D) requirements to reduce corporate overheads and optimize staffing levels means that Universities can utilize the opportunity and bid to supply this expertize. Universities also generate their own spin-outs from intellectual property they create, as well as licensing technology to industry, rather than transferring it.

In addition, some countries that supply a proportion of the funding to their academies, and who see collaboration between academia and industry as an increasingly critical component of an efficient local, regional, and national innovation system, have sought to develop policies that seek to facilitate this, and to make a contribution to local, regional, and national economic growth and development.

> Collaboration between universities and industries is critical for skills development (education and training), the generation, acquisition, and adoption of knowledge (innovation and technology transfer), and the promotion of entrepreneurship (start-ups and spin-offs). The benefits of university-industry linkages are wide-reaching: they can help coordinate R&D agendas and avoid duplications, stimulate additional private R&D investment (additionality effect), and exploit synergies and complementarities of scientific and technological capabilities. University-industry collaboration can also expand the relevance of research carried out in public institutions, foster the commercialization of public R&D outcomes, and increase the mobility of labor between public and private sectors [5].

2.2 Modes of Interaction Between the Academy and Industry

Industrial developments are generally supported by a number of possible approaches depending on the circumstances and those involved, and the perceived merits in the context of the objectives of the interaction.

Modes of interaction between the academy and industry can include the following.

- Consultancy—faculty member does external work for a company for which they are paid directly, though some institutions require a proportion to be given to the institution.
- Collaboration on an R&D project of mutual interest—where industry funds the R&D costs.
- Contract, or subcontract, from industry as part of an R&D project funded by industry, or by an external funding agency (e.g., EU, Fraunhofer, Innovate UK).
- Personnel exchange between the academy and industry.
- Setting up spin-off company—to generate product or service based on academy-owned Intellectual Property Rights (IPR).
- Licensing of academy-owned patents to industry.

These modes of operation are now analyzed in further detail.

2.2.1 Consultancy

Consultancy is normally under the direct control of the faculty though permissions may need to be sought from the institution on the time extent of the activity and also the ownership rights of any intellectual property that may be developed as part of the work. However, it does give the faculty member the opportunity to pursue areas of collaboration with industry in areas of their prime interests and where their research is at the leading edge. It also gives the companies involved the opportunity to outsource some of their R&D requirements to leading external authorities in the field without the overheads associated with setting up and maintaining an internal R&D section within the company. Also, in the development of a new product or service it may be difficult for the company to know in advance what R&D expertize will be optimum to further this goal. It thus becomes easier to buy in this expertize at the point that it is needed.

2.2.2 Collaborative Research and Development

Many institutions offer industry and government the opportunity to collaborate in areas of mutual interest and have set up frameworks, which define the rights and obligations of each party in the collaboration. It allows industry access to specialist expertize and also provides the academy with real-world experience in areas where a new product or service is a potential outcome of the collaboration. In addition, it allows the industrial partner(s) the opportunity to access specialist research expertize of the faculty in areas where some further investigations need to be done in leading-edge research areas before the project can be progressed (e.g., [6]).

Institutions have seen advantages in setting up Science and Technology Parks adjacent to the institution to act as a physical interface between the academy and industry, and to provide support for collaboration and innovation. Such collaboration may be local where the partners can benefit from physical co-location, but they can also be national and international where the collaborations can utilize broadband network technology where appropriate. Such Science and Technology Parks may also provide a supportive environment where new companies can be launched [7, 8].

The Confederation of British Industry (CBI) indicated in 2015 that [9]:

> More and more businesses of all sizes are benefiting from partnerships with universities for research, innovation, skills and professional development.
>
> The CBI refers to Hefce figures which show that in the three academic years up to 2012-13, the amount businesses spent on contract research – where universities have a customer/contractor relationship with companies – at higher education institutions grew at an annual rate of more than 6% to over £440 m. Companies also spent increasing amounts on consultancy services, use of facilities and equipment, and training and professional development – investing £400 m in 2012-13 [10].

HEFCE produced a Business and Community Interaction survey for 2012–2013 [11]. The CBI and Pearson Education also did a survey and reported as follows [12, 13]:

> A survey carried out by CBI and Pearson Education found that more than two thirds (70%) of the businesses had developed links of some kind with universities, while nearly half (48%) were looking to grow their university ties in the future.

Collaboration between the academy and industry may not always be straightforward due to the differences in culture and working practices between the two groups. The academy wishes to improve the standing of its research in terms of citations and league tables, whereas industry is focussed on its core business and maintaining its market share of products or services. Thus members of faculty are under pressure to work in areas of research that contribute directly to the esteem of the institution. However, the situation is changing due to a number of factors. These include:

- the trend to larger research collaborations with larger inter-institution grants, often in the leading institutions
- decline in research funding available due to economic constraints [for example UK research funding is below 0.5% of Gross Domestic Product (GDP)] [14]
- more directed forms of research, such as those concentrating on addressing what are perceived as "Grand Challenges" [15]
- perceived uncertainties about the future of UK collaborations within the European Union (EU).

The leading institutions, therefore, take a larger share of grant funding, which in turn forces other institutions to look at other options, including the local growth agenda and the application of knowledge to address local challenges and problems.

2.2.3 Contract or Sub-contract

Contracts from industry, funding agencies, or government may be allocated to academies in order to perform pieces of work or supply particular services. They may also be allocated to individuals within academies.

Larger projects funded by the European Union offer the opportunity for the academy and industry to collaborate with partners in other European Countries. Normally the evaluation of proposals is based on scientific excellence, industrial leadership, and the degree to which the proposal addresses key societal challenges. Successful grant proposals lead to a contract with the consortium to produce an agreed set of deliverables over a specific timescale, typically 3–5 years.

The recent decision by the UK to exit the EU has resulted in some uncertainty about how such collaborations involving the UK might proceed in the future. The UK government has already agreed to fund the UK cost for any proposals already approved, and it is envisaged that such funding would continue after the formal exit has been accomplished by 2018. Currently, Swiss partners participate in EU proposals and projects with their funding being paid automatically by the Swiss government.

The following report summarizes how the UK has performed in its relationship to EU funding since 2007 [16]:

> Headline facts from UK research and the European Union: The role of the EU in funding UK research include:
>
> - The UK is one of the largest recipients of research funding in the EU. UK scientists have earned more back in EU research grants (€8.8 bn, 2007 – 2013) than, analyses suggest, it has contributed to EU research expenditure (indicative figure of €5.4bn, 2007 – 2013, reported by the ONS).
> - The UK Government funds 30% of research and development undertaken in the UK, whilst the EU funds around 3%.
> - The UK is second only to Germany in terms of Framework Programme funding received (this is funding allocated competitively). If structural funds that are targeted at building research capacity in less economically developed regions of the EU are also taken into account, it is fourth.
> - The UK's world-class research talent is highly successful in securing much sought after EU European Research Council and Marie Sklodowska-Curie fellowships that are awarded on the basis of excellence – receiving just over a fifth and a quarter of the total budget respectively for these programmes.
> - EU funding represents an increasing proportion of research income for UK universities. Over the last five years, universities have seen their total research income rise thanks to a combination of EU and private sector funding. This is despite experiencing a drop in UK government funding over the same period.

2.2.4 Personnel Exchange

Exchanges between the academy and industry are supported by the Royal Academy of Engineering in the UK. It provided support for early to mid-career academics to spend 6–12 months in industry, and also visiting professorships to allow leaders from industry to work in academia [17, 18].

2.2.5 *Spin-off Companies*

Faculty can initiate spin-off companies with the support for facilitators inside or outside the University. They may belong to the person(s) who own the Intellectual Property Rights (IPR) and patents on any systems, products, or processes associated with the company. The University may own a percentage of the company—depending on the framework established within the institution.

2.2.6 *Licensing*

An institution may own some patents it does not wish exploit directly as it does not have the required infrastructure to do so without further investment of funds. If an external company is interested to utilize the patent(s) it may be possible to enter into a licensing arrangement with the institution for an agreed period.

These various models of operation may be summarised in Table 2.1.

2.3 Evaluation of the Pros and Cons of the Different Approaches

The pros and cons of the different approaches may be briefly summarized as follows:

> The many types of university-industry links have different objectives, scopes, and institutional arrangements (see Table 2.2). Collaboration may be more or less intense and may focus on training or research activities. Collaboration may be formal or informal, from formal equity partnerships, contracts, research projects, patent licensing, and so on, to human capital mobility, publications, and interactions in conferences and expert groups, among others [19]. Also it is useful to differentiate between short-term and long-term collaboration. Short-term collaborations generally consist of on-demand problem solving with predefined results and tend to be articulated through contract research, consulting, and licensing. Long-term collaborations are associated with joint projects and public-private partnerships (including private-funded university institutes or chairs, joint university-industry research centers, and research consortia), often allowing firms to contract for a core set of services and to periodically re-contract for specific deliverables in a flexible manner. Longer term collaborations are more strategic and open-ended, providing a multifaceted platform where firms can develop a stronger innovative capacity in the long run, building upon the capabilities, methods, and tools of universities [20, 21].

Table 2.1 Comparison of potential Aspects and Issues of the Models of Operation

Model	Ease of Setup	Timescale	Overhead	Potential Issues	Open Publication?
Consultancy	Dependent on faculty and institution	Variable	Institution may require a percentage	Reward model within the institution	Generally no
Collaborative R&D	Needs strong interest of both partners	Variable	May be none	EU projects required a minimum of 3 partners Dealing with IPR generated by a project	Yes
Contract or subcontract	Needs convergence of interests and expertize	Variable	May be none		Yes, by permission of the contractor
Personnel exchange	Needs convergence of interests and availability of suitable people for the roles	Typically one year	May be none		Yes
Spin-off company	Will require legal and administrative guidance	Variable	Institution may take a share of any subsequent sale, if written into the contact at setup	Takes time and effort, and generally employs its own staff—with faculty member remaining as an adviser	May be subject to nondisclosure
Licensing	Will require legal and administrative guidance	Variable	Institution may take a share of any revenue generated if it is part-owner of the patent(s)		Will need permission of the user of the license

The three university missions have given rise to the distinct concepts of teaching university, research university, and entrepreneurial university. University-industry collaboration may take place under all of these university regimes, although it will have a distinct focus on training in the teaching university, on R&D in the research university, and on technology commercialization and spin-offs in the entrepreneurial university. In any case, complementarities exist among the different university-industry links. For example, agreements to develop joint research may give rise to opportunities for training doctoral students. Likewise, collaboration in research may lead to the creation of spin-off companies or to the licensing of patents [23].

Table 2.2 A typology of university–industry links, from higher to lower intensity

Intensity of relationship	Components of the collaboration	Description of the components of the collaboration
High (relationships)	Research partnerships	Interorganizational arrangements for pursuing collaborative R&D, including research consortia and joint projects
	Research services	Research-related activities commissioned to universities by industrial clients, including contract research, consulting, quality control, testing, certification, and prototype development
	Shared infrastructure	Use of university labs and equipment by firms, business incubators, and technology parks located within universities
Medium (mobility)	Academic entrepreneurship	Development and commercial exploitation of technologies pursued by academic inventors through a company they (partly) own (spin-off companies)
	Human resource training and transfer	Training of industry employees, internship programs, postgraduate training in industry, secondments to industry of university faculty and research staff, adjunct faculty of industry participants
Low (transfer)	Commercialization of intellectual property	Transfer of university-generated IP (such as patents) to firms (e.g., via licensing)
	Scientific publications	Use of codified scientific knowledge within industry
	Informal interaction	Formation of social relationships (e.g., conferences, meetings, social networks)

Source Adapted from Perkmann and Walsh [22], Tables 2 and 3

Table 2.3 illustrates how the priorities for university–industry partnerships can be affected by the particular stage in the academic and economic development of the university.

2.4 Challenges, Cultural and Social Issues Between the Academy and Industry

The following issues may characterize differences at the interface between the academy and industry, and highlight the ongoing issues which can affect the degree to which a collaboration between the academy and industry is able to progress and be successful.

Table 2.3 Priorities for university–industry partnerships at different stages of economic development along the three missions of universities

Mission of University	Most developed countries	Least developed countries
Teaching University	• Private participation in graduate programs • Joint supervision of Ph.D. students	• Curricula development to improve undergraduate and graduate studies • Student internships
Research University	• Research consortia and long-term research partnerships to conduct frontier research	• Building absorptive capacity to adopt and diffuse already existing technologies • Focus on appropriate technologies to respond to local needs
Entrepreneurial University	• Spin-off companies, patent licensing • Entrepreneurship education	• Business incubation services • Entrepreneurship education

Source [24]

2.4.1 Timescale

The academy normally operates on a longer timescale than industry. Historically, research projects in the academy have lasted for up to three years or more. Larger, inter-University projects may last up to five years. Industry on the other hand is often in a competitive situation in the market place and needs to deliver products and services on a much shorter timescale in order to maintain its position. There can also be tensions between short-term technological progress and longer term research on what are regarded as the more important fundamental questions (called “Grand Challenges” in some disciplines).

2.4.2 Reward Model

The academy reward model has traditionally been based principally on the delivery of new research results, which have been published in peer-reviewed journals and conferences. The results have therefore been assessed by national and international experts in the field against the current state of the art. In recent years some universities have widened these criteria to include excellence in teaching and collaboration with industry. However in the latter area, the extent and merit of the work done can be difficult to evaluate if it is subject to confidentiality agreements and non-disclosure. In addition, where it is able to be evaluated, there is currently no generally accepted scale of excellence against which it may be measured and evaluated (except perhaps in the area of patents). This can introduce uncertainty in assessing the value of what has been achieved.

2.4.3 Value of Applied Research

Historically, the academy has regarded pure research as of a higher value than applied research, and regarded the latter as more concerned with development or implementation rather than seeking to discover something fundamentally new. However, this is also slowly changing over time. The academy is increasingly recognizing that often pure and applied research go hand in hand, particularly in engineering and medical areas [25].

2.4.4 Technology Transfer Culture

Some institutions have a long history of working with industry and have a strong entrepreneurial culture. They have been able to provide avenues of opportunity for undergraduates and graduates to obtain employment with companies with whom the academy has strong links and associations. However, this can cause some undergraduates to leave before completing their course. This can benefit industry, but may not be in the long-term interests of the individual.

2.4.5 Communication and Values

Communication and decision-making in the academy has been historically collegiate in nature and based on an informal consensus within the faculty. The faculty determines the overall academic direction of the institution. On the other hand, industry is often more hierarchical and may require the formal approval by senior management of any decisions that are made. Thus, there can be considerably more freedom and flexibility within the academy to change direction relatively quickly, if this should be required. This may be more difficult to accomplish in industry. There can also be differences in the stated values of the respective organizations which can give rise to misunderstanding. However, there are current trends toward an increasing degree of management and control within the academy in order to meet the strategic priorities as determined by its mission. This can enable the academy to align more closely to the needs and requirements of industry.

2.4.6 Differences Across Discipline Areas

Disciplines in the applied sciences lend themselves more naturally to exploitation by industry because they are closer to industrial products and services. On the other hand, subjects in the liberal arts and the humanities may appear to be more distant, and consequently less applicable. This asymmetry between disciplines can create tension in the academy when its mission includes technology transfer or improvement of society in general. The academy can give different internal priories to its various academic disciplines with corresponding financial and budgetary implications. However, such divisions are often not clear-cut as many companies employ arts graduates in various roles, including in the humanizing of technology, and producing products and services which are adaptable and easy to use. In addition, the creative industries offer opportunities for interdisciplinary collaborations between technology and the arts.

2.4.7 Economic Impact

Impact factors have been incorporated into research grant proposals and the periodic audit of research quality in the UK. This has been opposed by key academics in the UK. More than 18,000 academics, including six Nobel Prize Winners, have written to the UK government to condemn the current plans to include economic impact in the evaluation of research.

> The scholars are concerned that making university research more accountable to the wider economy will stifle the sort of curiosity-driven research that has led to groundbreaking discoveries and Nobel prizes".
>
> History shows us that in many cases it is basic research, undertaken purely out of curiosity to understand more about our world, that has delivered revolutionary breakthroughs, "Dr Kirby-Harris said." X-rays, lasers and semiconductors – technologies widely used in every aspect of our lives – all stem from discoveries made through fundamental research, undertaken without any immediate application in mind.
>
> Sir Tim Hunt, one of six Nobel Prize winners to sign the petition, said: "The impact guidelines will discourage academics from making discoveries and will encourage people to come up with unoriginal research proposals. The whole idea of research is to find out things you didn't know before. The fruits of basic research are unpredictable and to seek to control them in this way is not in the interests of the country [26, 27].

2.4.8 Diversification of Academic Mission

The academy supports the principal areas of teaching, research, knowledge transfer, and widening access. Some concentration of mission might have been expected according to the history of an institution and its strengths, but the external environment can also have an influence. For example, institutions that have extensive research grants and do best in the delivery of research results, generally have the best potential for collaboration with industry. They have the best infrastructure and are able to provide the best support for these collaborations. Lesser institutions can end up by being squeezed out of both research and knowledge transfer. Thus diversity of mission can be as much affected by merit and attractiveness to the market place as by internal choice.

Further detail on these issues and the potential differences between the academy and industry can be found in [2].

2.4.9 Intellectual Property Agreements

Intellectual property agreements need to be carefully drafted in order to avoid potential future problems. There needs to be a clear and unequivocal understanding on both sides of what the agreement is and the entitlements of the partners in the agreement. Clearly they need to be considered well in advance of the production of any patents.

2.5 Lessons Learned

The tensions that a number of faculties have felt between basic research and working with industry is not easy to resolve and is likely to continue. Historically the academy has been more concerned with blue-sky research, i.e., scientific research in areas where real-world applications are not necessarily apparent. In addition, where applied research is performed, there has always been a tendency in the academy to regard it as of lesser value (or even or no value) compared to basic research. It has been characterized as "development" or "implementation" and not regarded as research. The periodic research audits that are performed (e.g., in the UK via the REF) need to ensure that the evaluation of applied research and outcomes of academy–industry collaborations do full justice to the work that has been done, and do not regard it as a lesser achievement simply because it is more difficult (for commercial and confidentiality reasons) to secure open literature publications in internationally leading journals (and which can count up to 60% in the overall evaluation).

The trend toward increasing contact with industry along with increasing direction by the university executive was not universally accepted by academia. For example, the Congregations of the universities of Oxford and Cambridge voted against proposals for increasing the managerialism in their institutions in 2006. It was regarded as a threat to the traditional autonomy within their colleges [28]. The academy was not against reform per se, but was of the view this was better handled by academic leadership within the colleges and with due regard for their academic freedom, democracy, and independence, rather than the executive and/or trustees of the university. The primary issue, therefore, was to decide the form of governance which would best serve the interests of the university and those of the faculty, bearing in mind their historical traditions. Nevertheless both Oxford and Cambridge have developed strong collaborations with industry in areas of mutual interest both before and after the debates on the optimal form of governance within the institution. Thus these collaborations were not intrinsically dependent on the form of governance that was chosen. However, clearly large amounts of time and resource were spent on the debate which appeared to lead directly, or indirectly, to the resignation of the Chief Executive Officer of Oxford (the Vice chancellor). With the benefit of hindsight this can have done little to maintain morale or reduce the tension between management and faculty over issues such as this. However, Oxford was ranked first in the global league table position of universities in 2016 [29], so it has not affected its overall reputation and standing as an institution, and may have enhanced it.

2.6 Conclusions

Models of interaction between the academy and industry have been reviewed. Different models may be appropriate for the particular mission of an academy, and the different phases of development of academies over time. Local and national governments are seeking to influence the contributions that universities may be able to make to local and national economies in the areas of economic growth and the development of new products and services.

The following is an extract from "Making industry-university partnerships work—Lessons from successful collaborations" [30]:

> Long-term strategic partnerships between universities and industry that run for 5 to 10 years are the most productive at driving innovation, according to a study published by the Science/Business Innovation Board AISBL, a not-for-profit scientific association create to improve the climate for innovation in Europe.
>
> Universities and industry have been collaborating for over a century, but the rise of a global knowledge economy has intensified the need for strategic partnerships that go beyond the traditional funding of discrete research projects.
>
> World-class research universities are at the forefront of pioneering such partnerships. They are designed to run longer, invest more, look farther ahead and hone the competitiveness of companies, universities and regions.
>
> In short, they transform the role of the research university for the 21st century, anchoring it as a vital center of competence to help tackle social challenges and drive economic growth.

Further Reading

Bridgeford, T., St Amant, K.: Academy-Industry Relationships and Partnerships: Perspectives for Technical Communicators (Baywood's Technical Communications Series), p. 260, Routledge, Abingdon (2015)

Brown, R.: Everything for Sale? The Marketisation of Higher Education., p. 256, Routledge, Abingdon (2013)

Caves, R.: Creative Industries: Contracts Between Art and Commerce, p. 464. Harvard University Press, Cambridge, MA (2002). (New Edition 2nd & Subsequent)

Etzkowitz, H.: The Triple Helix: University-Industry-Government Innovation in Action, p. 176. Routledge, Abingdon (2017)

Larsen, K., Bandara, D.C., Esham, M., Unantenne, R.: Promoting University-Industry Collaboration in Sri Lanka: Status, Case Studies, and Policy Options (Directions in Development—Human Development), p. 96. World Bank Publications, Washington DC (2016)

McGettigan, A.: The Great University Gamble: Money, Markets, and Higher Education, p. 230. Pluto Press, London (2013)

Mowery, D., Nelson, R., Sampat, B., Ziedonis, A.: Ivory Tower and Industrial Innovation: University-Industry Technology Before and After the Bayh-Dole Act (Innovation & Technology in the World Economy), p. 257. Stanford University Press, Stanford, CA (2004)

References

1. http://www.hefce.ac.uk/rsrch/funding/business/
2. Earnshaw, R.A.: Knowledge exchange, technology transfer and the academy. In: Dill, J. C., Earnshaw, R.A., Kasik, D.J., Wong, P.C. (eds) Expanding the Frontiers of Visual analytics and Visualization. pp. 469–480. Springer, London, ISBN 978-1-4471-2803-9 (2012). http://link.springer.com/chapter/10.1007%2F978-1-4471-2804-5_26#page-1
3. Earnshaw, R.A.: Research and Development in Art, Design and Creativity. p. 100, Springer, Switzerland (2016). http://dx.doi.org/10.1007/978-3-319-33005-1
4. Clark, B.R.: Creating Entrepreneurial Universities: Organizational Pathways of Transformation, p. 180. International Association of Universities and Elsevier Science, Bingley, UK (1998)
5. http://innovationpolicyplatform.org/sites/default/files/rdf_imported_documents/PromotingUniversityIndustryCollaborationInDevelopingCountries.pdf
6. http://ocr.yale.edu/faculty/collaborating-industry
7. https://en.wikipedia.org/wiki/Science_park
8. https://en.wikipedia.org/wiki/List_of_science_parks_in_the_United_Kingdom
9. http://www.cbi.org.uk/news/best-of-both-worlds-coverage/
10. https://www.theguardian.com/higher-education-network/2015/jan/27/businesses-up-their-investment-in-uk-university-research-projects
11. http://www.hefce.ac.uk/pubs/year/2014/201410/
12. http://www.cbi.org.uk/cbi-prod/assets/File/Education-and-skills-survey-2015.pdf
13. https://www.theguardian.com/higher-education-network/2015/jan/27/businesses-up-their-investment-in-uk-university-research-projects
14. https://www.theguardian.com/science/occams-corner/2015/mar/13/science-vital-uk-spending-research-gdp, http://faseb.org/Science-Policy-and-Advocacy/Federal-Funding-Data/NIH-Research-Funding-Trends.aspx, https://www.timeshighereducation.com/news/universities-decline-charity-research-grants-due-fall-public-funding
15. http://grandchallenges.org/
16. https://royalsociety.org/news/2015/12/UK%20research%20and%20EU/
17. http://www.raeng.org.uk/grants-and-prizes/schemes-for-people-in-industry
18. http://www.ncbi.nlm.nih.gov/books/NBK45046/
19. Hagedoorn, J., Link, A.N., Vonortas, N.S.: Research partnerships. Res. Policy **29**, 567–586 (2000)
20. Koschatzky, K., Stahlecker, T.: New forms of strategic research collaboration between firms and universities in the German research system. Int. J. Technol. Transfer Commercialization **9**, 94–110 (2010)

21. http://innovationpolicyplatform.org/sites/default/files/rdf_imported_documents/PromotingUniversityIndustryCollaborationInDevelopingCountries.pdf
22. Perkmann, M., Walsh, K.: University-industry relationships and open innovation: Towards a research agenda. Int. J. Manage. Rev. **9**(4), 259–80 (2007). https://spiral.imperial.ac.uk/bitstream/10044/1/1396/1/Perkmann%20Walsh%202007.pdf
23. http://innovationpolicyplatform.org/sites/default/files/rdf_imported_documents/PromotingUniversityIndustryCollaborationInDevelopingCountries.pdf
24. http://innovationpolicyplatform.org/sites/default/files/rdf_imported_documents/PromotingUniversityIndustryCollaborationInDevelopingCountries.pdf
25. Shneiderman, B.: The New ABCs of Research: Achieving Breakthrough Collaborations. Oxford University Press, Oxford, pp. 336 (2016)
26. http://www.independent.co.uk/news/science/nobel-laureates-dont-put-money-before-science-1860138.html
27. http://www.nybooks.com/articles/archives/2011/jan/13/grim-threat-british-universities/
28. http://www.independent.co.uk/news/education/higher/mutiny-at-oxford-526959.html, http://www.bloomberg.com/news/articles/2005-12-04/shaking-up-oxford, http://broom02.revolvy.com/main/index.php?s=John%20Hood%20(university%20administrator), http://www.ft.com/cms/s/0/b9e99bd8-72bb-11db-a5f5-0000779e2340.html?ft_site=falcon&desktop=true#axzz4MQwKRMBB
29. http://www.ox.ac.uk/news/2016-09-21-oxford-ranked-first-among-global-universities
30. http://www.sciencebusiness.net/Assets/94fe6d15-5432-4cf9-a656-633248e63541.pdf, http://www.sciencebusiness.net/ourReports/reportDetail.aspx?ReportId=33

Chapter 3
Technology Transfer for the Creative Industries and Wider Industrial Applications

Abstract The creative industries require innovative and added-value content. They cover a variety of market sectors including advertising, architecture, art, crafts, design, fashion, film, music, performing arts, publishing, R&D, software, toys and games, TV and radio, and video games. They are increasingly driven by digital content and distributed via digital networks. They can have a significant impact on economies through wealth and job creation, and also serve a valuable social and cultural purpose. They often require interdisciplinary expertize in order to successfully integrate technology and art and design. This leads to the importance of developing supportive environments, which are able to foster interdisciplinary developments. To enable this in today's context, interoperability is increasingly required across a variety of platforms and products to ensure customers are able to seamlessly access content and services. Access to content requires metadata and open standards. Transaction processing involves digital currency and easy-to-use licensing and commerce. In addition, facilitation of new and wider creative applications arising from research and development in science, engineering, and technology have an increasing role to play in support of a nation's growth and development. The exploitation of knowledge and information is the key to economic progress. The academy can play a key role in this enterprise in collaboration with industry.

Keywords Digital content · Metadata · Open standards · Transaction processing · Digital currency · Intellectual property · Licensing · Wealth creation · Cultural engagement · Industrial applications · Creative technologies

3.1 Introduction

Creative industries are at the intersection of the arts, culture, business, and technology and utilize creativity, knowledge, technical facility, and information. They trade with assets in the form of intellectual property and have the potential to generate jobs, revenue, and cultural engagement. They can also promote social

R. Earnshaw, *Research and Development in the Academy, Creative Industries and Applications*, SpringerBriefs in Computer Science,
DOI 10.1007/978-3-319-54081-8_3

inclusion, cultural diversity, and human development and so can serve a social and cultural relations purpose, in addition to wealth creation.

Ideas and information are able to be transformed into cultural goods and services through a group of linked activities, often utilizing digital technologies. Digital tools and techniques may be utilized in content creation, and may also be used as part of the transport service or delivery mechanism. Products and services also need to be viable in an increasingly globally competitive environment which seeks innovation and added value. This requires creativity, skill, talent and innovation across a wide variety of sectors. Digital convergence is bringing together IT, telecommunications, and media—enabling user access to a wide variety of content and services on a variety of platforms and in a multitude of ways: in particular, the opportunity for interactivity, both in games paradigms and in more novel ways, represents a radically new approach to media that is growing in significance. Creating innovative collaborations across a number of different sectors requires interdisciplinary skills in design and implementation. The growth of data and transactional processing present a major challenge in order for them to be useful for consumers and businesses.

The creative industries are estimated to have a significant impact on economies through wealth and job creation. The UK's creative industries are now worth a record £84.1 billion to the UK economy, according to data published on 26 January 2016. The UK's Creative Industries grew by 8.9% in 2014—almost double the UK economy as a whole [1, 2].

One definition of the creative industries would include the following areas—advertising, architecture, art, crafts, design, fashion, film, music, performing arts, publishing, R&D, software, toys and games, TV and radio, and video games [3].

In 2015, the UK Department of Culture, Media and Support identified the following creative sectors [4] (the computer games sector is also important):

1. Advertising and marketing
2. Architecture
3. Crafts
4. Design: product, graphic and fashion design
5. Film, TV, video, radio, and photography
6. IT, software and computer services
7. Publishing
8. Museums, galleries, and libraries
9. Music, performing and visual arts.

Combining the above areas, and noting that some areas may receive a part or whole public subsidy via regional or national governments, whereas others do not and operate on a commercial basis, is illustrated in Table 3.1.

The production of creative content generates the value, which can be made available to consumers via sale or subscription. Agencies and distributors may also be involved and benefit from licensing arrangements for their contributions.

Table 3.1 Creative industries and public subsidy

Possible public subsidy in whole or part	Commercial operation
Film	Advertising and marketing
TV	Architecture
Radio	Crafts
Museums, galleries, libraries	Design: product, graphic and fashion design
Music, performing and visual arts	Computer and video games

3.2 Challenges and Opportunities

The creative industries face a unique mixture of both challenges and opportunities because of their combination of disciplines and varied backgrounds of the practitioners and researchers. Working within their own particular disciplines, researchers will typically find it comfortable and familiar to develop and evaluate ideas and processes utilizing the methodologies that are traditionally associated with, or are intrinsic to, their discipline. The challenges and opportunities occur where cross-disciplinary and interdisciplinary work takes place [5]. This leads to two issues relating to research and development: first, how to effectively support and nurture cross and inter disciplinary research in the creative industries, and second, how to measure success, impact, and output in such developments.

Creative industries are by definition closer to the market because they involve the generation of products and services, which meet a customer requirement or business need. Innovate UK's Creative Industries Strategy 2013–16 identified three key themes offering innovation challenges and opportunities to drive growth for the UK's creative and digital businesses. These are convergence, data, and transaction. Convergence implies that service interoperability is required across a variety of platforms and products to ensure customers are able to seamlessly access content and services. The growth of data increasingly requires digital ways of analysis and presentation in order for it to be useful for consumers and businesses. In addition, access to content requires metadata and open standards. Transaction processing involves digital currency and easy-to-use licensing and commerce [6, 7].

> The creative industries are a well-known success story in the UK, employing 1.4 million and worth more than 5% of GDP. As well as their direct economic value these industries play an important role in catalysing innovation across the wider economy, through new ideas, products, services and ways of working [8].

> Of these 1.4 million, 232,000 or around 16.5%, are employed in the design sector in the UK. The UK has a multi discipline design sector, from strategic design to brand design. According to a Department for Business, Innovation and Skills report, for every £1 invested in design provides an average return on investment of £25. The UK government has demonstrated its belief that design helps businesses succeed by investing €1.3 m on design leadership support in 2012 – one of the greatest investments in a design support programme in Europe [9].

A number of Case Studies included in this volume illustrate how research and development translate into practical products and services.

3.3 Properties of Creative Industries

According to Caves [10], creative industries are characterized by seven economic properties:

1. *Nobody knows principle*: Demand uncertainty exists because the consumers' reaction to a product are neither known beforehand, nor easily understood afterward.
2. *Art for art's sake*: Workers care about originality, technical professional skill, harmony, etc., of creative goods and are willing to settle for lower wages than offered by 'humdrum' jobs.
3. *Motley crew principle*: For relatively complex creative products (e.g., films), the production requires diversely skilled inputs. Each skilled input must be present and perform at some minimum level to produce a valuable outcome.
4. *Infinite variety*: Products are differentiated by quality and uniqueness; each product is a distinct combination of inputs leading to infinite variety options (e.g., works of creative writing, whether poetry, novel, screenplays or otherwise).
5. *A list/B list*: Skills are vertically differentiated. Artists are ranked on their skills, originality and proficiency in creative processes and/or products. Small differences in skills and talent may yield huge differences in (financial) success.
6. *Time flies*: When coordinating complex projects with diversely skilled inputs, time is of the essence.
7. *Ars longa*: Some creative products have durability aspects that invoke copyright protection, allowing a creator or performer to collect rents

3.4 Wider Industrial Applications

Following World War II, there was increasing recognition that science, engineering, and technology were able to contribute significantly to a nation's growth and development. In the USA, atomic power, radar, nylon, penicillin, and computers had already demonstrated the power of research combined with engineering skills [11–14]. It was perceived that such research and development was essential in the treatment of disease, and the creation of new products, industries and jobs. Thus, basic research that was funded by philanthropy and a limited number of private donors was unlikely to yield the potential benefits that could be achieved. What was needed was a co-ordinated programme of research and development at national level achieved by government, industry, and the expanding network of universities and research laboratories. This was achieved and resulted in significant advances in many areas including medicine, computers, and the human exploration of space [11, 12]. However, "computers" have undergone several metamorphoses that have essentially created new devices that had relatively little in common with their predecessors (e.g., mainframe—minicomputer—PC—mobile/tablet). In addition, the output from the academy of graduates and postgraduates with advanced knowledge and skills was able to provide industry with the continued expertize necessary to further advance its areas. Although the world has also changed significantly over this period resulting in increased global competition—the basic premise of the importance of research and development has remained the same. Other countries have benefited from the licensing of technology and open research publications, and invested similarly in their own advanced education and infrastructure to generate new skills and technology. Increased travel and communication has resulted in the international flow of people, capital, and ideas. The exploitation of knowledge and information can result in economic benefits to all those involved (Research and development are also essential for addressing major longer term issues such as climate change, energy supply, and genetic modification of crops, as well as issues that are a priority for developing countries).

In 2014 the UK committed [15]:

> £5.9billion capital to support scientific excellence out to 2021: the most long-term commitment to science capital in decades. And ….strengthening our partnerships between the public and private sector, epitomised by the Industrial Strategy and the 8 Great Technologies
>
> 8 Great Technologies:
>
> 1. Big data and energy-efficient computing: The data deluge will transform scientific inquiry and many industries too.
> 2. Satellites and commercial applications of space
> 3. Robotics and autonomous systems: We can already see that this is a general purpose technology with applications ranging from assisted living for disabled people through to nuclear decommissioning.
> 4. Synthetic biology: Modern genetics has emerged in parallel with the IT revolution and there is a direct link – genetic data comes in digital form. The future is the convergence of "dry" IT and "wet" biological sciences. One of the most ambitious examples of this is synthetic biology – engineering genes to heal us, feed us, and fuel us.
> 5. Regenerative medicine will open up new medical techniques for repairing and replacing damaged human tissue.
> 6. Agri-science: Although genetics is above all associated with human health, advances in agricultural technologies can put the UK at the forefront of the next green revolution.
> 7. Advanced materials and nano-technology: Just as we understand the genome of a biological organism so we can think of the fundamental molecular identity of an inorganic material. Here too we can increasingly design new advanced materials from first principles. This will enable technological advances in sectors from aerospace to construction. Quantum photonics is an exciting area where advanced materials and digital IT converge.
> 8. Energy and its storage: One of the most important applications of advanced materials is in energy storage. This and other technologies will enable the UK to gain from the global transition to new energy sources

The Organisation for Economic Co-operation and Development (OECD) stated [16] that:

> The ability to create, distribute and exploit knowledge has become a major source of competitive advantage, wealth creation and improvements in the quality of life. Some of the main features of this transformation are the growing impact of information and communications technologies (ICT) on the economy and on society; the rapid application of recent scientific advances in new products and processes; a high rate of innovation across OECD countries; a shift to more knowledge-intensive industries and services; and rising skill requirements.

The Computing Community Consortium convened a round-table of industry and academic participants in July 2015 to better understand the landscape of industry–academic interaction, and to discuss possible actions that might be taken to enhance those interactions.

The principal conclusions were as follows [17]:

> In reflecting on the results of the survey and the roundtable discussions, below are some concrete actions that could be taken to enhance the future vitality and impact of academic–industry interactions:
>
> (1) Establish a means of measuring and benchmarking industry/academic interactions. It is hard to assess or improve something that cannot be measured. Create a repository of best-practices for industry/university interactions.
> (2) Recognize that there is a need for career paths that may combine elements of a traditional academic career in a university research and education setting with career paths that involve significant time within a new or established company, and create mechanisms that support such career paths.
> (3) Consider ways that advanced infrastructure can be made widely available to the research community. Finding ways to make advanced computing and devices, large data sets, and unique facilities more widely available will benefit industry (it will create "power-users" for their infrastructure), academic research (avoiding wasted time and resources replicating capabilities already in existence), and education (students will learn on the latest and greatest).
> (4) Convene a long-term forum or body around industry academic interaction. Collaborations between academia and industry will continue to play a central role in the transfer of long-term and fundamental research into the US economy. Recognizing and supporting this transfer will provide mutual benefits to all stakeholders.

3.5 Interdisciplinary Collaboration

Shneiderman [18] advances the case for combining applied and basic research and a new paradigm for interdisciplinary collaboration that puts engineering and design on an equal footing with basic science. Dill et al. [19] detail how the Boeing Company collaborated with the academy on the development of visual analytic tools.

Advancing interdisciplinary research is a major challenge and the current difficulties were outlined in [20]. However, there are increasing signs that the importance of interdisciplinary research and development is being recognized in leading institutions. The provost of Massachusetts Institute of Technology (MIT) indicated that MIT's success in achieving its fifth position in the World University Rankings in 2016 was principally due to its interdisciplinary approach, which was fostered through interdepartmental laboratories, shared facilities and initiatives centred on global problems. Working across disciplinary boundaries in a collaborative way enabled faculty and students to see opportunities that might not otherwise be seen if they were working in a disciplinary silo. In addition, the interdisciplinary approach was also implemented at undergraduate level, where all undergraduates were required to take at least one humanities or social sciences subject per semester, regardless of their specialism [21, 22].

Nevertheless, obtaining funding for interdisciplinary research proposals can still be difficult simply because such proposals may fall outside the traditional expertize of grant awarding bodies. In addition, evaluators may be unsure whether the proposers are leaders in their fields or not, and also whether the work is innovative or not. There are also few highly ranked multidisciplinary journals, so it is difficult to get published and establish a peer-reviewed track record in a multidisciplinary area [23–25].

3.6 Lessons Learned

Digital technologies can facilitate smaller scale production and collaboration rather than competition. However, competition can also produce innovation.

The success of the creative industries sector has generated renewed interest in the arts sector and the creativity they can express, and the potential for the future. The products and services that have been generated nationally and internationally can have a significant economic impact on a country's financial performance.

In turn, the academy needs to understand and support interdisciplinary environments, and provide appropriate structures and financial support within the academy to facilitate this. The academy also needs to be alert to partnering opportunities with local and national industry in order to realize the potential of its creative assets through networks of partners, and the collective opportunities that they can provide.

Research and development in science, engineering, technology and medical areas, can produce significant new compounds and materials that can translate into major commercial products and services with a global impact when effectively partnered with industry. Examples of this are graphene [26, 27], and also one of the largest spin-off sales from the academy (at £200 million) of a pharmaceutical process to determine the size of powdered particles in drug design [28].

3.7 Conclusions

The creative industries are increasingly driven by digital content and distributed via digital networks, and are estimated to have a significant impact on economies through the generation of revenue and jobs. A globally competitive environment seeks innovation and added value in products and services. This requires creativity, skill, talent and innovation across a wide variety of disciplinary sectors. This raises the challenge and opportunity of interdisciplinary collaborations. Digital convergence is bringing together IT, telecommunications, and media—enabling user access to a wide variety of content and services on a variety of platforms and in a multitude of ways.

Science, engineering, and technology have an increasing role to play in support of a nation's growth and development. Therefore, technology transfer from the academy to industrial applications is an important component of the future. However, the academy must be alive to the need to be innovative and, in particular, to embrace the opportunities of interdisciplinarity. There is no more important interdisciplinary arena than the arts–technology interface, where radically new tools are changing the nature of art, but rich creative design is also essential to making new-technology products attractive and beneficial for clients.

Further Reading

Caves, R.E.: Creative Industries: Contracts between Art and Commerce, p. 464. Harvard University Press, Harvard, MA (2002)

Davies, R.: Introducing the Creative Industries, p. 280. Sage Publications Ltd, London (2013)

Flew, T.: The Creative Industries—Culture and Policy, p. 248. Sage Publishing, London (2012). https://uk.sagepub.com/en-gb/eur/the-creative-industries/book233058

Henley, D.: The Arts Dividend: Why Investment in Culture Pays, p. 192. Elliott & Thompson, London (2016)

Hewison, R.: Cultural Capital: The Rose and Fall of Creative Britain, p. 288. Verso Books, London (2014)

Howkins, J.: The Creative Economy: How People make Money from Ideas, p. 304. Penguin, London (2013)

McRobbie, A.: Be Creative: Making a Living in the new Culture Industries, p. 224. Polity Press, Cambridge, UK (2015)

Shneiderman, B.: The New ABCs of Research: Achieving Breakthrough Collaborations, p. 336. Oxford University Press, Oxford (2016)

The Future of Computing Research: Industry-Academic Collaborations. p. 24 (2016). http://cra.org/ccc/wp-content/uploads/sites/2/2016/06/15125-CCC-Industry-Whitepaper-v4-1.pdf

Metadata Standards and Organization. *NCSU Libraries* (2008)

National Information Standards Organization (NISO) A Framework of Guidance for Building Good Digital Collections (PDF) (3rd ed.). Baltimore, USA: NISO. ISBN 978-1-880124-74-1 (2007)

National Information Standards Organization (NISO) Understanding Metadata (PDF). NISO Press, Bethesda, USA. ISBN 978-1-880124-62-8 (2004)

References

1. https://www.gov.uk/government/news/creative-industries-worth-almost-10-million-an-hour-to-economy
2. https://www.gov.uk/government/statistics/creative-industries-economic-estimates-january-2016
3. Howkins, J.: The Creative Economy: How People Make Money From Ideas, pp. 88–117. Penguin, London. ISBN: 9780141977034 (2013). https://www.penguin.co.uk/books/196214/the-creative-economy/
4. Department for Culture, Media & Sport—Creative Industries Economic Estimates January 2015. (PDF). https://www.gov.uk/government/uploads/system/uploads/attachment_data/file/394668/Creative_Industries_Economic_Estimates_-_January_2015.pdf (2015)
5. Earnshaw, R.A., Liggett, S., Heald, K.: Interdisciplinary Collaboration Methodologies in Art, Design and Media. Proceedings of International Conference on Internet Technologies and Applications, pp. 381–388, ISBN 978-0-946881-81-9 (2013). http://scim.brad.ac.uk/staff/pdf/raearnsh/Collaboration%20Methodologies%20-%20Final.pdf
6. https://connect.innovateuk.org/web/creativektn/article-view/-/blogs/technology-strategy-board-launches-creative-industries-strategy-2013-16
7. https://www.gov.uk/government/uploads/system/uploads/attachment_data/file/362253/Creative_Industries_Strategy_2013-16.pdf
8. https://connect.innovateuk.org/web/creativektn/article-view/-/blogs/technology-strategy-board-launches-creative-industries-strategy-2013-16
9. https://connect.innovateuk.org/web/design-sig/article-view/-/blogs/case-study-film-design-in-innovation
10. Caves, R.E.: Creative Industries: Contracts between Art and Commerce, p. 464. Harvard University Press, Harvard, MA. ISBN 9780674008083 (2002). http://www.hup.harvard.edu/catalog.php?isbn=9780674008083, http://www.stuartglover.com.au/wp-content/uploads/2011/09/2002-Creative- Industries-Contracts-between-Art-and-Commerce2.pdf
11. Bush, V.: Science, The Endless Frontier. National Science Foundation, Washington DC, 1945 (reprinted 1990). http://www.nsf.gov/od/lpa/nsf50/vbush1945.htm, https://archive.org/details/scienceendlessfr00unit, http://sciencepolicy.colorado.edu/admin/publication_files/2010.24.pdf
12. Science, Technology and the Federal Government: National Goals for a New Era. https://www.nap.edu/read/9481/chapter/1 (1993)
13. Smith, B.L.R.: American Science Policy since World War II. The Brookings Institution, Washington DC (1990). https://books.google.co.uk/books/about/American_science_policy_since_World_War.html?id=C8baAAAAMAAJ&redir_esc=y
14. President's Council of Advisors on Science and Technology, Renewing the Promise: Research Intensive Universities and the Nation. US Government Printing Office, Washington DC. https://catalog.hathitrust.org/Record/002628066 (1992)
15. UK Plan for Growth: Science and Innovation. https://www.gov.uk/government/uploads/system/uploads/attachment_data/file/387780/PU1719_HMT_Science_.pdf (2014)
16. http://www.oecd.org/science/sci-tech/1918259.pdf
17. The Future of Computing Research: Industry-Academic Collaborations. p. 24 (2016). http://cra.org/ccc/wp-content/uploads/sites/2/2016/06/15125-CCC-Industry-Whitepaper-v4-1.pdf
18. Shneiderman, B.: The New ABCs of Research: Achieving Breakthrough Collaborations, p. 336. Press, Oxford University, Oxford. ISBN 9780198758839 (2016)
19. Dill, J.C., Kasik, D.J., Darvill, D.J.: Case study: successful deployment of industry-university collaborative visual analytics research. 46th Hawaii International Conference on System Sciences, IEEE Computer Society, pp. 1505–1511. doi:10.1109/HICSS.2013.126 (2013). https://www.computer.org/csdl/proceedings/hicss/2013/4892/00/4892b505.pdf
20. Earnshaw, R.A.: Research and Development in Art, Design and Creativity, p. 87. Springer, Cham, Switzerland. Sections 3.1 (pp 32–33), 5.2.5 (pp 74–75). ISBN 978-3-319-33005-1. doi:http://dx.doi.org/10.1007/978-3-319-33005-1, http://www.springer.com/gb/book/978331933 0044 (2016)

21. https://www.timeshighereducation.com/news/world-university-rankings-2016-2017-results-announced
22. http://web.mit.edu/nuclearpower/pdf/nuclearpower-summary.pdf
23. https://www.timeshighereducation.com/news/multidisciplinary-research-career-suicide-junior-academics
24. https://www.timeshighereducation.com/news/multidisciplinary-study-gets-lip-service-not-cash/420266.article
25. Goldin, I., Kutarna, C.: Age of Discovery: Navigating the Risks and Rewards of the New Renaissance, p. 272. Bloomsbury Information Ltd., London. ISBN-13: 978-1472936370 (2016)
26. http://www.graphene.manchester.ac.uk/explore/the-story-of-graphene/
27. http://www.stfc.ac.uk/about-us/our-impacts-achievements/case-studies/accelerating-the-development-of-graphene/
28. https://www.timeshighereducation.com/news/spin-off-sold-for-200m/156751.article

Chapter 4
The Entrepreneurial Academician and the Collaborating Industrialist

Abstract A vision for the future of computing and digital media relies on Moore's Law for increased speed and functionality in the areas of processing, memory, and telecommunications. Most of the key advances which are driven by technology, and are commercializable, are able to take advantage of these factors. This is demonstrated by a review of how technology development and innovation has taken place in the recent past. In a number of cases this innovation has been performed primarily by one or more individuals in academia or industry, though they may have received help and support in the setting up of a company. The general motivations for collaboration on the part of industry and the academy are identified. The capabilities and skills of the academic entrepreneur and the collaborating industrialist are reviewed. The characteristics of an academy/industry project are analyzed and a set of criteria are proposed for evaluating a project in real time. A threshold is considered above which collaboration can successfully take place, and below which it cannot. In addition, possible side effects of collaboration are reviewed.

Keywords Moore's law · Digital convergence · Project monitoring and evaluation · Entrepreneurship · Spin-off company · Technology transfer offices · Business incubators · Innovation parks · Venture capital

4.1 Introduction

Moore's law states that overall processing power for computers doubles every 1.5–2 years, or less [1]. This also applies to telecommunications. Although a general guide rather than a fundamental law, it has proved remarkably consistent since the implementation of the first semiconductor integrated circuit in 1960 (Fig. 4.1).

It is expected that for the immediate future, Moore's Law will ensure that computational power will continue to increase at current rates, bringing more speed

R. Earnshaw, *Research and Development in the Academy, Creative Industries and Applications*, SpringerBriefs in Computer Science,
DOI 10.1007/978-3-319-54081-8_4

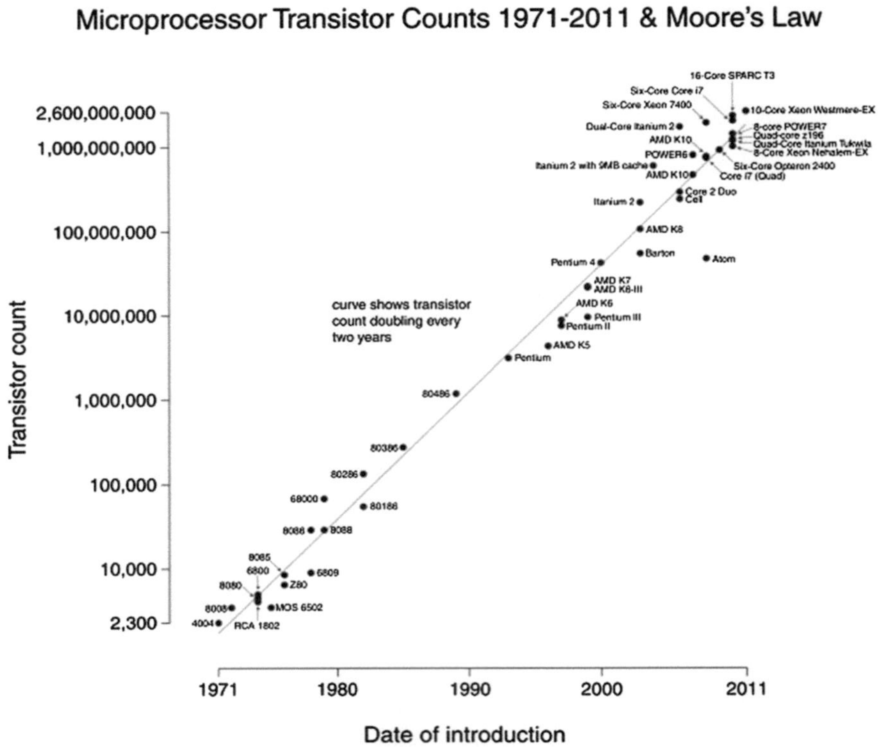

Fig. 4.1 Plot of CPU transistor counts against dates of introduction. Note the logarithmic vertical scale; the line corresponds to exponential growth with transistor count doubling every two years. *Source* http://en.wikipedia.org/wiki/Moore%27s_law. It is copied under the license Creative Commons Attribution-Share Alike 3.0 Unported. https://commons.wikimedia.org/wiki/File:Transistor_Count_and_Moore%27s_Law_-_2011.svg

and capacity to handle more sophisticated applications and end-user requirements. Devices are becoming increasingly intelligent and are able to monitor data and environment. Automobiles can contain up to 100 microprocessors to monitor the various functions of a car. New cars carry 200 lb of electronics with over a mile of wiring. On a wider front, the Internet of Things is able to connect together embedded devices that can provide a wide variety of data and sensor information. Gartner [2] estimates that there will be 26 billion devices on the Internet by 2020. A network of autonomous smart devices will enable a whole range of operations and applications to be carried out without direct intervention by the user.

Utilization of digital media systems and the increase in the use social media appears to follow the law of sharing, an equivalent of Moore's law in the context of social media. The law of sharing states that the average amount of shared information doubles every year [3]. The analogy helps businesses to be aware of the rapidly changing environment in which they are operating, and enables them to define business information handling requirements, and develop and accelerate commercial and social applications, where appropriate.

4.2 The Challenge for the Academician

Garcia-Martinez outlines some of the difficulties and challenges for the academician [4]:

> Even for academics with the right set of skills, university culture can be a strong deterrent. Traditional science education doesn't embrace entrepreneurship, so many young scientists feel unqualified. Principal investigators often take the view that Ph.D. students and postdocs should focus entirely on research. Another disincentive is that, in too many departments, patents and startup companies may count for little during hiring and promotion.
>
> Even in a supportive environment, the challenges of doing both at once—becoming a world-class researcher and commercializing a technology—are so formidable that many early-career scientists come to see them as insurmountable.
>
> These are real limitations, but let's consider some inspiring facts. The number of patents, licenses, and spin-off companies created by academics is increasing. According to a study published in 2009 by researchers at the Massachusetts Institute of Technology (MIT) Sloan School of Management, alumni from MIT had created 25,800 active companies with worldwide annual sales of $2 trillion. These days, many universities support budding academic entrepreneurs through ad hoc courses and access to technology transfer offices, business incubators, and innovation parks.
>
> Early-career scientists can find role models among the many prolific academics who have become successful entrepreneurs, including biochemist Herbert Boyer, who co-founded Genentech, and chemist George Whitesides, who co-founded Genzyme and many other companies from his academic bases at MIT and Harvard University. Every year, the MIT Technology Review "35 Innovators Under 35" (TR35) program recognizes talented scientists who pursue groundbreaking business ideas, at an early stage in their career. Among past awardees is Shwetak Patel of the University of Washington in Seattle, who won an award for designing simple sensors for monitoring electricity consumption in domestic environments. Another winner is Luis von Ahn of Carnegie Mellon University in Pittsburgh, Pennsylvania, who won a TR35 award for using "captchas" to help digitize books.
>
> As a former TR35 awardee myself and a member of the jury for the last 3 years, I have come to believe that to make the leap into entrepreneurship one needs three prerequisites: solid research, a good idea about how to turn findings into a business opportunity, and a supportive environment

Table 4.1 Integrating the Entrepreneurial academician and the collaborating industrialist

Creative idea	Implementation	Company founded	Pioneer(s)
Design by computer	Architecture machine	MIT Media Lab, 1973	Nicholas Negroponte
Simulation, 3D graphics	Vector, colour display	Evans and Sutherland, 1968	David Evans/Ivan Sutherland
Mass use of PCs	PC operating software	Microsoft, 1975	Paul Allen/Bill Gates
Quality, aesthetics, interaction	Visual interface	Apple, 1976	Steve Jobs/Steve Wozniak
3D computing and visualization	3D hardware and software	Silicon Graphics, 1982	Jim Clark
Motion pictures—3D animation by computer	3D animation hardware and software	Pixar, 1986	Ed Catmull/Alvy Ray Smith
3D graphics and gaming	Graphics processing units and system on a chip	Nvidia, 1993	Jen-Hsun Huang et al.
Web content	Web browser	Netscape, 1994	Jim Clark/Marc Andreessen
Organize the world's information and make it universally accessible and useful	Search results available within <0.2 s	Google, 1998 3.5 billion searches per day	Larry Page/Sergey Brin
Sharing information	Online social media	Facebook, 2004 1.65 billion users, 2016	Mark Zuckerberg
Video upload and download	Video servers	YouTube, 2005 1 billion views per day	Chad Hurley
Short messages (up to 140 chars)	Online social networking service	Twitter, 2006, 310 m monthly active users	Jack Dorsey et al.
Online photo sharing	Online social media service	Instagram, 2010 300 m users Dec 2014	Kevin Systrom/Mike Krieger
Image messaging	Multimedia mobile app	Snapchat, 2011, 100 m daily active users; 6 billion video views per day	Evan Spiegel et al.
Video messaging, Vlog	Creative take	Vlog, 5 m users Beme, 2015	Casey Neistat/Matt Hackett

4.3 The Integration of Entrepreneurship and Industrial Development

In the pioneering of new areas, it is possible for both the initial idea and its first implementation to be performed by the same people (though not necessarily to run the company that is established). Table 4.1 summarizes some key creative ideas and the companies that were formed to implement them. In a number of cases this involved the key people who pioneered the particular area and its development, though often others were also involved in the initial setup of the company. Thus there were two principal aspects to the development. The first was to see the potential of the creative idea—often at the state of the art—and how it could form the basis of an implementation and meet a user need in the market place. The second was to understand how best to make it work at scale in the real world. A key driver in many of these examples is technology and how it was utilized, as well as access to venture capital.

Over the time period covered by Table 4.1 there were significant developments in the power and functionality of integrated circuits and software. More power and capacity was increasingly available at lower cost. This applied both to computing and also to telecommunications. This in turn facilitated digital convergence and also the provision of large-scale online servers. Latterly this has extended to offering supercomputing facilities in the cloud.

Many of the state-of-the-art developments in technology that subsequently formed the basis for a commercial company arose in association with faculty and students in Stanford University. Silicon Valley has one of the highest proportion of start-up companies. The proximity of venture capital facilitates this process.

4.4 Deutsche Telekom Laboratories

The Deutsche Telekom Laboratories identified that the growing competition in consumer markets was forcing industry to explore new ways to foster product and service innovations. Key factors in any collaboration were felt to be as follows [5]:

Table 4.2 Attributes of industry and the academy

Industry attributes	Academy attributes
Sourcing latest technological advances	Enhancement of teaching
Laboratory usage	Funding/financial resources
Personnel resources/cost savings	Source of knowledge and empirical data
Risk sharing for basic research	Political pressure
Stabilising long term research projects	Enhancement of reputation
Recruiting channel	Job offers for graduates

Table 4.3 Company priorities and motivations

Company priority	Motivation
Primary reasons	• Open-up innovation • Sourcing latest technological advances
High	• Constant renewal of know-how • Recruiting channel
Medium	• Risk sharing for basic research • Stabilizing long-term research projects
Low	• Cost savings • Laboratory usage

Source 4 qualitative and quantitative Interviews with DT Laboratories Founder and 3 members of the current management team [5]

Table 4.4 Difficulties in the collaboration

Category of difficulty	Difficulties
Cultural	• Divergent missions and goals • Conflicting interests concerning secrecy and IPR • Different nature of work
Institutional	• Different languages and assumptions • Divergent perception of what the "product" of R&D is • Structure change and change of responsibilities on the company's side
Operational	• Lack of knowledge about the partner and his processes • Insufficient coordination and project management • Lack of acceptance for results generated by the partner

Source 4 qualitative and quantitative Interviews with DT Laboratories Founder and 3 members of the current management team [5]

- Co-ownership collaboration frameworks are a powerful means to overcome cultural, institutional, and operational collaboration barriers
- Building a common vision for the collaboration is key in overcoming the cultural barriers
- Recruiting employees with background in the partners' domain is the most powerful means to overcome operational barriers.

The general motivations for collaboration on the part of industry and the academy were identified as shown in Table 4.2.

The specific motivations for the collaboration of Deutsche Telekom are identified in Table 4.3.

The difficulties encountered in the collaboration are summarized in Table 4.4.

Solutions for the difficulties in the collaboration are identified in Table 4.5.

Table 4.5 Solutions to the difficulties

Category of difficulty	Solutions
Cultural	• Employment of post-docs that have a natural interest in application orientated R&D work • Defined publication and IPR policies • Co-location, biyearly off-sites, one central coffee shop, transparency policy
Institutional	• Organization according to focus of work in strategic research and innovation development • Clearly defined deliverables, different KPIs in strategic research and innovation development, initial productization or even spin-off support for researchers • Stability through separated organization with allocated staffing
Operational	• Clearly defined processes • Coordination through quarterly project reviews and progress presentations • NIH-Syndrome reduced through mutual projects
Implications for practitioners	• Creation of a mutually shared mission and shared goals • Creation of an environment of trust and transparency • Clear policy on publication and IPRs • Co-location, shared and open office space, and team building activities • Clear division of labour and management with different key performance indicators (KPIs)

Source 4 qualitative and quantitative Interviews with DT Laboratories Founder and 3 members of the current management team [5]

4.5 Thresholds for Successful Collaborations

Is there a threshold above which collaboration can successfully take place, and below which it cannot? What are the key factors that need to be considered? Possible aspects include the following:

- Motivation for the collaboration
- The intensity of the collaboration
- The degree of innovation the collaboration can produce.

Is there a threshold which causes other knock-on effects? One study of industry collaborations identified the following issue [6].

> We report findings from a unique longitudinal dataset on all the researchers in all the engineering departments of 40 major universities in the UK for the last 20 years. We introduce a new measure of industry collaboration based on the fraction of research grants that include industry partners. Our results show that productivity increases with the intensity of industry collaboration, but only up to a certain point. Above a certain threshold, research productivity declines. Our results are robust to several econometric estimation methods, measures of research output, and for various subsamples of academics.
>
> Our results for this panel indicate that the number of publications increases with the presence of non-collaborative funding and increases even further with the intensity of

Table 4.6 Parameters of academy–industry collaboration

Category of the project	Parameter of the project
Project definition	• Objectives and deliverables • Motivating factors for the project • Transdisciplinary considerations • Advance on the state of the art • Potential for innovation • Expected impact—scientific, technological, economic, competitive, and social terms (where relevant) • Meeting the needs of the market place • Environmental and social impact
Work plan	• Team coherence and effectiveness • Complementarity of partners and skills • Allocation of tasks and resources • Project milestones • Project integration
Resources required	• Funding for staff and researchers • Researcher expertise required • Equipment required and access • Strength of the collaboration
Location of the collaboration	• Physical proximity of project and partners
Organization and management	• Partner collaboration agreement • Project management • Project manager • Structures, procedures, and reporting • Communication strategy • Risk management • Research data • Steering Committee • Dissemination and publication agreements • Information that should be disseminated to policy makers, the scientific community, the general public, a specific group of end users • Exploitation and market opportunities • IPR agreements • Non-disclosure agreement • Involvement of potential users and stakeholders? • Links with cognate projects • Are there any ethical, policy-related/regulatory, safety or gender issues? • Are there any beneficiaries?

industry collaboration, but only up to a certain point. For levels of collaboration above 30%–40%, research output declines. These results have proven robust to variations in the econometric estimation method, for various subsamples of academics, and for various measures of academic research output. Nevertheless, some remarks are in order. Basic research output and average publication quality are significantly positively affected by (non-collaborative) funding but are not significantly affected by industry collaboration.

4.6 Parameters of Academy–Industry Collaboration

A number of indicators may be used to measure performance in collaborations [7]. These are detailed in Table 4.6.

The parameters in Table 4.6 may be used to evaluate a collaborative project at design and implementation stages. They may also be used for real-time assessment of the progress of the project.

4.7 Lessons Learned

The academic entrepreneur and the innovative industrialist can both establish successful companies. In collaboration, the sum can be greater than that of the individual parts. The academic may find that productivity increases with the intensity of industry collaboration, but with a limit. For levels of collaboration above 30–40%, it has been noted that research and publication output in the academy declines. This may not be in the long-term interests of an academic who wishes to remain in the academy. However, for those who wish to transfer from the academy to industry, this would not normally constitute an issue.

In general it has been recognized that although the faculty member whose idea is embedded in the start-up may wish to be CEO, a better overall result is normally obtained by bringing in an experienced industry CEO to take the new company forward. This is because they are able to take a wider and more objective view of the company as a whole, and take business decisions which are in the best interests of the company and its development and growth. In addition, pump-priming the company is likely to need venture capital. An experienced CEO is best placed to handle this, and also to provide the reputational basis to be able to secure venture capital. One possible role for the faculty member is chairman of the board, or adviser to the company.

4.8 Conclusions

Many of the start-up companies summarized in Table 4.1 arose out of faculty and/or students at Stanford University. Thus it is clear that both the university and the adjacent Silicon Valley provided a fruitful environment for migrating state-of-the-art creative ideas into innovative products and services. However, other high technology hubs are developing in various geographical areas in the USA, including San Diego, Los Angeles, Denver, and Seattle [8–10].

Further Reading

Catmull, E.: Creativity Inc: Overcoming the Unseen Forces That Stand in the Way of True Inspiration, p. 368. Bantam Press, London (2014)

Clark, B.R.: Creating Entrepreneurial Universities: Organizational Pathways of Transformation, p. 180. Pergamon, Oxford (1998)

Clark, J.: Netscape Time: The Making of the Billion Dollar Start Up, p. 276. St Martin's Press, New York (1999)

Gold, S.: Steve Jobs: The Biography & Lessons of the Mastermind behind Apple, p. 104. CreateSpace Independent Publishing Platform (2016)

Kirkpatrick, D.: The Facebook Effect: The Real Inside Story of Mark Zuckerberg and the World's Fastest Growing Company, p. 384. Virgin Books, London (2011)

Lecuyer, C.: Making Silicon Valley: Innovation and the Growth of High Tech, 1930–1970, p. 424. MIT Press, Cambridge, MA (2005)

Negroponte, N.: Towards a theory of architecture machine. J. Archit. Educ. **4**. http://cyberneticzoo.com/wp-content/uploads/2010/10/Architecture_Machine_Negroponte.pdf (1969)

Negroponte, N.: Architecture Machine, p. 164. MIT Press, Cambridge, MA (1970)

Negroponte, N.: Being Digital, p. 249. Coronet Books, London (1996)

Schmidt, E., Rosenberg, J.: How Google Works, p. 305. John Murray, London (2015)

Schmidt, E., Cohen, J.: The New Digital Age: Reshaping the Future of People, Nations, and Business, p. 368. John Murray, London (2014)

Shattock, M.: Entrepreneurialism in universities and the knowledge economy: Diversification and Organizational Change in European Higher Education, p. 256. Open University Press, London (2008)

Stearn, A.: Make Instagram Work for Your Business: The Complete Guide to Marketing Your Business, Generating Leads, Finding New Customers, and Building Your Brand, p. 144. CreateSpace Independent Publishing Platform (2014)

Therin, F.: Handbook of Research on Techno-Entrepreneurship: How Technology and Entrepreneurship are Shaping the Development of Industries and Companies, p. 369. Edward Elgar, Cheltenham, UK (2013)

Vise, D.A.: The Google Story, p. 352. Pan, London (2008)

References

1. Moore, G.E.: Cramming more components onto integrated circuits. Electron. Mag. http://arstechnica.co.uk/wp-content/uploads/sites/3/2016/03/gordon_moore_1965_article.pdf (1965)
2. Gartner Says the Internet of Things Installed Base Will Grow to 26 Billion Units By 2020. http://www.gartner.com/newsroom/id/2636073 (2013)
3. Boutin, P.: The Law of Online Sharing. MIT Technology Review. http://www.technologyreview.com/review/426438/the-law-of-online-sharing/ (2011)
4. Garcia-Martinez, J.: The Third Way: Becoming an Academic Entrepreneur. Science. http://www.sciencemag.org/careers/2014/03/third-way-becoming-academic-entrepreneur (2014)
5. Rohrbeck, R., Arnold, H.M.: Making university-industry collaboration work a case study on the Deutsche Telekom Laboratories. http://www.rene-rohrbeck.de/documents/Rohrbeck_Arnold_(2006)_University-Industry-Collaboration_Presentation.pdf (2006)

6. Banal-Estanol, A., Jofre-Bonet, M., Meissner, C.: The Double-Edged Sword of Industry Collaboration: Evidence from Engineering Academics in the UK. City University, Dept of Economics, Discussion Paper No 13/03. https://www.city.ac.uk/__data/assets/pdf_file/0004/201676/13_03_indcollab03_08_2013wp.pdf, http://openaccess.city.ac.uk/id/eprint/2916 (2013)
7. Rossi, F., Rosli, A.: Indicators of university-industry knowledge transfer performance and their implications for universities: evidence from the UK's HE-BCI survey. Centre for Innovation management Research, Working Paper No 13, Birkbeck College. http://www.bbk.ac.uk/innovation/publications/docs/CIMR-WP-13.pdf (2013)
8. http://mashable.com/2016/05/17/emerging-tech-hubs/#81gH6CQBEkq1
9. http://blog.indeed.com/2016/07/06/is-silicon-valley-still-top-tech-hub/
10. http://www.inc.com/jessica-stillman/the-7-easiest-cities-to-get-your-start-up-funded-that-aren-t-san-francisco.html

Chapter 5
Case Study: Shared Virtual and Augmented Environments for Creative Applications

Alexei Sourin

Abstract The origin of shared virtual worlds is summarized. They were predicted by many novelists as well as envisaged in blockbuster movies at the start of the computer era. Constructing the first shared virtual worlds began in the last decade of the twentieth century when the Internet became ubiquitous. Extensions of the hypertext mark-up language (HTML) to immersive 3D graphics were proposed by several vendors and research groups that eventually materialized into what we know now as Extensible 3D (X3D) and its predecessor Virtual Reality Modeling Language (VRML). Academia has capitalized on these new horizons for education by setting up virtual campuses in Active Worlds—online shared virtual worlds based on the Renderware rendering engine. Thousands of virtual citizens populated CyberTown—a 3D online community developed in VRML language and the Blaxxun collaborative platform. The beginning of the new Millennium saw a start to many new developments and paradigms ranging from massively multiplayer online role-playing games (MMORPG) to serious networked gaming and simply living in virtual reality. New development tools, new businesses, and new psychological, ethical, and judicial problems had arrived. Second Life had a major impact on the field as the countries were opening their embassies there, and international corporations used to set up their offices for interviewing job applicants. For many years, Sony Computer Entertainment Inc. was exploring how useful their very own networked virtual world "PlayStation Home" could be. However only a small fraction of the billions of Internet browsing users were involved in virtual 3D living—and these were mostly content creators. Virtual 3D cities were implemented in Google StreetView which brought together augmented reality (AR) and a global positioning system (GPS) in mobile devices. Internet gaming using AR has become a "national sport" and the most popular leisure activity for young people in some countries. Tourists have become accustomed to utilizing AR and GPS navigation in the places they visit. All these new opportunities of "being concurrently here and elsewhere" with mobile phones, just a click away, are encapsulated in Pokémon Go. Its impact is analyzed. The future for shared VR and AR is summarized.

R. Earnshaw, *Research and Development in the Academy, Creative Industries and Applications*, SpringerBriefs in Computer Science,
DOI 10.1007/978-3-319-54081-8_5

Keywords Virtual reality · Augmented reality · Cyberspace · Metaverse · Shared virtual environments · Shared worlds · Cyberworlds · VRML · X3D · e-learning · Cybereducation

5.1 Inspiration

The idea of "parallel worlds" which exist in virtual spaces supported by interconnected computers was always very popular among novelists and movie creators, even before the time when the Internet had become ubiquitous. The term cyberspace, which is about objects and identities existing within the computing network, was coined by William Gibson in his novel "Neuromancer" [1]—one of the seminal works in the *suberpunk*[1] genre. In the same book the term "matrix" is used as a dataspace. Meanwhile, Neal Stephenson in "Snow Crash" in 1992 [2] describes the shared virtual world Metaverse where humans use their virtual representations—avatars—to interact with each other, as well as with robots in a 3D virtual replica of the real world. In 1981, similar concepts were used in the novel "True Names" [3] by Vernor Vinge. "Labyrinth of Reflections" (1997) [4]—the first novel of cyberpunk trilogy written by the very popular Russian science fiction writer Sergey Lukyanenko—goes deep into technological and ethical problems of living in a digital "Deeptown" populated by "Divers." Divers wear special cybernetic body suites to connect all the human senses to common networked environments.

5.2 Technology

In computer science, virtual reality (VR) replicates a real environment by means of 3D computer-generated imagery which enables the user to move around in the virtual environment and interact with objects. It can also support touch and audio data [5–8]. The environment can be displayed by means of a VR headset, a projector screen, or a 3D Cave. When the 3D environment replicates the appearance and properties of the real world, it can be used for a variety of purposes. These include architectural design, engineering design, military training, fashion design, treatment of phobias, visualization, heritage, healthcare training, and simulation [9]. It enables training procedures to be carried out in a safe and secure environment.

[1]Cyberpunk is a subgenre of science fiction that features advanced science and technology in an urban, new-future dystopian society. It pictures advanced technological and scientific achievements in information technology and cybernetics as well as conflicts between some powerful mega-corporations and private security forces on one side, and underworld of illegal trade, gangs, drugs, etc. on the other side. Classic cyberpunk characters are marginalized, alienated loners who live on the edge of society where daily life is impacted by rapid technological changes, ubiquity flow of computerized information, and invasive cybernetic modification of the human body.

For example, a flight simulator [10] replicates the same environment as a real aircraft and it is thus able to test the proficiency and competence level of a pilot in carrying out a variety of maneuvres for certification purposes. Such tests could be expensive and time-consuming to perform in the real world, as well as being potentially dangerous if not carried out correctly. In the virtual world, mistakes can be made and these can contribute to the training experience. A 3D environment that represents an artificial world can be used for distance learning, multiuser online gaming and other creative entertainment applications.

Augmented reality (AR) comprises a view of the real world which also contains computer-generated elements superimposed upon it such as audio, graphics, video, or location data [11, 12]. It thus provides an enhanced view of reality. An example is a helmet for a construction worker which displays information about the construction site on a see-through screen which is overlaid on the worker's view of the real site. This could be the architectural plans, or information about the building materials being used. Such information may be transmitted by radio signals from a central computer. If location information is also used (such as GPS), then the part of the physical site being viewed can be linked directly to its component parts in the virtual view, so there is a one-to-one correspondence between the real and the virtual as the worker moves through the building site. These views can also be shared with other people by means of the radio link. Another example is the recent trial of lightweight and unobtrusive Google Glass, an optical head-mounted display in the form of eye glasses, and Leap Motion controller which allows for overlaying the actual image of the hands with their 3D skeleton model.

5.3 Prediction

Movie makers helped to envisage full immersion in shared and augmented virtual worlds in many movies, including "The Lawnmover Man" (1992), "The Thirteenth Floor" (1999), "The Matrix" (1999), and "Divergent" (2014). However most of the ideas and technologies presented in these films are still mainly in the future. On the other hand, the direct hand interaction shown in "Minority Report" (2002) has preceded today's human–computer interaction using optical capturing devices such as Microsoft Kinect and Leap Motion controllers. Augmenting real and virtual worlds, as demonstrated in "Iron Man" (2008) and "Kingsman: The Secret Service" (2014), is also progressing successfully with affordable gadgets such as Oculus Rift and the Sony Virtual Reality Headset, while the developers are eagerly anticipating the arrival of the Microsoft HoloLens for making further advances in this area. Fantastic neural connection Tsaheylu shown in "Avatar" (2009) is now triggering new ideas in the area of brain–computer interaction while the electroencephalogram (EEG) reading devices have become wireless and quite affordable (Fig. 5.1).

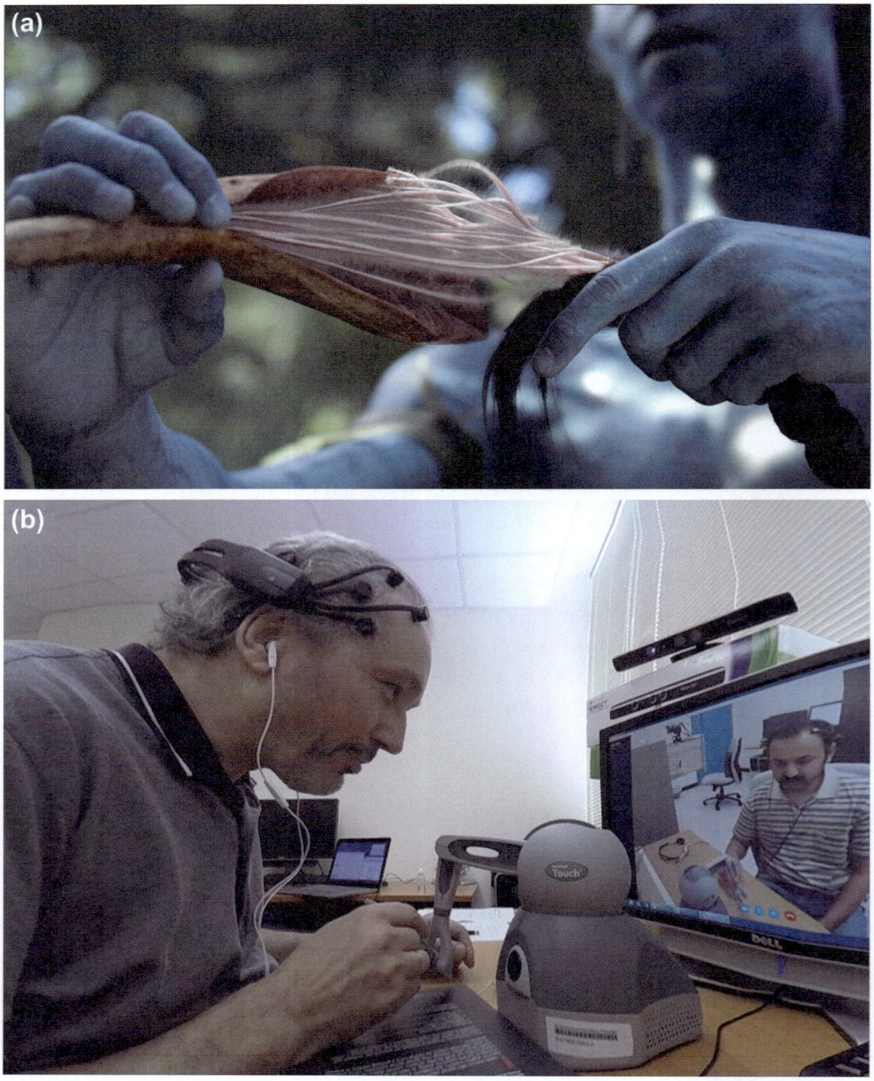

Fig. 5.1 **a** Neural connection Tsaheylu shown in "Avatar." **b** The author wearing EEG device while interacting in cyberspace

5.4 Evolution

One of the first implementations of shared VR was done in Habitat—a multiplayer online game initially created in 1985 by Randy Farmer and Chip Morningstar and made available for a beta test in 1986 by Quantum Link, an online service for the Commodore 64 computer. Habitat computers communicated via modems and telephones over a commercial packet-switching network though a mainframe host system. The participants could see a real-time animated display of activities in Habitat including avatars of other participants and could exchange text messages with each other. The whole virtual community was governed by its citizen—the participants—while the host maintained the Habitat model, enforced the rules and informed the participants about the state of the shared environment. The networked interaction was of most interest for the Habitat creators and even in this rather primitive shared world, the avatars had to find a way to survive and live better, they could be even robbed or destroyed by other avatars. Habitat was run by Lucasfilm from 1986 to 1988. It was then relaunched in 1988 with much improved graphics as Club Caribe on Quantum Link as well as Fujitsu Habitat in Japan in 1990. The Japanese version then was further reincarnated in 1995 into WorldsAway which was closed down in 2014 known as Dreamscape.

The arrival of Windows 3.11 in 1993 had made the Internet a universally available tool, and, consequently, it initiated setting up further virtual worlds in cyberspace, some of which still exist till today with their devoted inhabitants. Faculties and students of universities have eagerly moved to explore new horizons for education by setting up virtual campuses in Active Worlds—an online shared virtual world based on using Renderware rendering engine. Active Worlds went through a series of changes of owners, and also business schemes ranging between free and paid access. However, it had an attractive user interface and API which allowed thousands of users to create, easily visit, and actively participate in 3D virtual spaces. Though initially created mostly as a 3D browsing environment to replace traditional web pages, it attracted the attention of educators as a new teaching platform which could both replicate existing educational practice as well as create new educational environments which are impossible, or very costly, to make and maintain in real life (Fig. 5.2a). Under the growing demand from teachers and university professors, as well as distance and lifelong learners, Active Worlds organized an entire educational universe which was named Active Worlds Educational Universe or AWEDU. Active Worlds remains one of the oldest surviving commercial 3D environment technology with thousands of dedicated users.

Another notable pioneer among shared virtual worlds was CyberTown (Fig. 5.2b). It started in 1997 as Colony City—a showcase project of Blaxxun Interactive of Munich, Germany. It used the Virtual Reality Modeling Language (VRML)[2] for creating the content which was shared among the networked

[2]Virtual Reality Modeling Language (VRML) and its current successor Extensible 3D (X3D) are ISO standard file formats for describing interactive 3D objects and virtual worlds. They are designed to be used on the Internet, intranets, and local client systems. They are also intended to be universal interchange formats for integrated 3D graphics and multimedia. VRML and X3D are capable of representing static and animated dynamic 3D and multimedia objects with hyperlinks to other media such as text, sounds, movies, and images. VRML and X3D are following *declarative programming style*, i.e. they tell the computer *what to do*. It differs from the *imperative programming style*, like in C and in a popular graphics library OpenGL, which tell the computer *how to do* things. VRML and X3D are maintained by Web3D Consortium—international, non-profit, member-funded, industry standards development organization founded in 1997.

(a)

(b)

Fig. 5.2 Screenshots of **a** one of the Active Worlds and **b** CyberTown login page

computers using the Blaxxun Community Platform—a server which allowed the participants to see each other's avatars, the shared 3D environments, as well as exchange text messages, and maintain their own spaces and personal data. By 1999, it has become CyberTown which offered the visitors the option of being 3D guests, who could walk around and chat, or to take some responsibilities, for example in the form of jobs earning a daily wage in CityCash. The CyberTown citizens could use this virtual money to buy 3D houses and other commodities. The citizens with more technical experience could make their own objects using VRML, place them in their houses as well as sell them in the CyberTown's Mall to make extra CityCash. This was interesting: to live a virtual life, to have a virtual house, and have their virtual identity in this CyberTown, while at the same time having an existence in the real world. Creative visitors could make their own appearance by designing their own avatars. After visiting somebody's house, there was the illusion that indeed one has just been somewhere and seen interesting things like interactive tropical aquariums, trained cyberdogs, animated sculptures, or could be teleported with the host to a yacht near Sunset Beach—one of the CyberTown places available for visitors. Other public places of CyberTown existed as 3D chat rooms and places for various activities like selling/buying things, sending virtual money to other citizens, etc. The environment was very much driven by the administrators and the visitors had to follow the rules, however it did become popular, and visitors enjoyed themselves by creating and sharing interesting virtual items and their own avatars. With its own dedicated users, the system managed to exist till 2012, even after it started to charge citizens a small annual membership fee, and the CyberTown citizens still have a hope that it will be reincarnated soon or later.

The technologies used in making CyberTown propagated to many other projects creating a variety of virtual worlds available for visiting on the web. VRML offered many technological solutions, and it was a convenient and freely available tool for both solving problems of 3D visualization on a personal computer without requesting expensive resources, and for placing 3D content on the web. For many years, Blaxxun Interactive allowed the free use of their server for setting up simple shared spaces. It also offered a commercial license for setting up advanced shared environments based on the infrastructure and business model of CyberTown. In 2000, the author created his own virtual space using VRML and Blaxxun platform. It was a virtual multiuser replica of Nanyang Technological University in Singapore [13] with all its buildings and interiors of the lecture theaters, tutorial rooms, and student dormitories. It followed Singapore time regardless of where the visitors are coming from—the day lasts from 7:00 am to 7:00 pm, as it is always in Singapore. The avatars of the student bots populating the virtual campus move to the educational buildings during the daytime, and in the evening all the activity shifts to dormitories. Like CyberTown, the virtual Campus of NTU fluctuated in its popularity, and it is still available for visiting, however it is more like a virtual time machine for traveling to the Nanyang Technological University, as it was 15 years ago.

5.5 Maturity

The beginning of the new Millennium provided a start to many new developments in shared VR. Many new exciting virtual spaces had been created with millions of regular users who either come to "live" in these parallel universes enjoying meeting avatars of other people, owing interesting pieces of property, and even making some profit there (e.g., Habbo, There, Second Life, Entropia Universe, Meez, World of Kaneva), or playing what are termed massively multiplayer online role-playing games (MMORPG)[3] which are available for all ages (e.g., Ultima Online, EverQuest, World of Warcraft, MapleStory, Phantasy Star Online, Guild Wars, Disney Club Penguin, Whyville, Webkinz, Mokitown).

Initially the popularity of Second Life caused reputable news agencies to send their reporters to highlight new happenings in this virtual shared world. In addition, countries were opening their embassies there, and international corporations set up their offices for interviewing job applicants. Second Life is an online virtual world, developed by Linden Lab, based in San Francisco, and launched in 2003 (Fig. 5.3a). At the time of writing, Second Life has approximately 1 million regular users. Second Life world can be accessed free of charge using either Linden Lab's own client programs, or via alternative third-party viewers. Second Life users (residents) may create avatars representing themselves. They can explore the world (known as the grid), meet other residents, socialize, participate in individual and group activities, build, create, shop, and trade virtual property and services with one another. It is a platform that principally features 3D-based user-generated content. Second Life also has its own virtual currency—the Linden Dollar—which is exchangeable with real-world currency. The residents can build their own objects using a built-in three-dimensional modeling tool, as well as use a procedural scripting language—Linden Scripting Language—which can be used to add interactivity to objects. In addition to this, external software can be used for importing polygon meshes, textures, animations, and gestures into the Second Life environment. Started as yet another virtual world, Second Life soon changed their mode of operation promoting the idea that this virtual world is managed by the users themselves and leaving the administrators to a supporting role which is mostly invisible. It immediately attracted thousands of virtual residents who came to this virtual land as pioneers to develop, explore, and even to become as virtually rich and successful as Anshe Chung[4] who had become an iconic symbol for the economic opportunities that the virtual world offered to its residents. For many people,

---

[3]Massively multiplayer online role-playing games (MMORPGs) are a combination of role-playing video games and massively multiplayer online games in which a very large number of players interact with one another within a shared virtual world. In MMORPG, the player usually assumes the role of some fictional character and takes control over many of that character's actions. The players may form teams to achieve a common goal. The roles in the team differ depending on the game. While progressing through the game, the players acquire new weapons, avatars and other items which form their personal inventories. MMORPG are usually exchanging events between the participating computers which update the status of the virtual world as it is seen by each individual player. MMORPGs are played throughout the world.

[4]Anshe Chung is an avatar in the online world Second Life. Referred to as the "Rockefeller of Second Life" by a CNN journalist, she has built an online business involving development, brokerage, and arbitrage of virtual land, items, and currencies. According to Chung, in June 2004 she began selling and creating custom animations and then used this money to buy and develop virtual land.

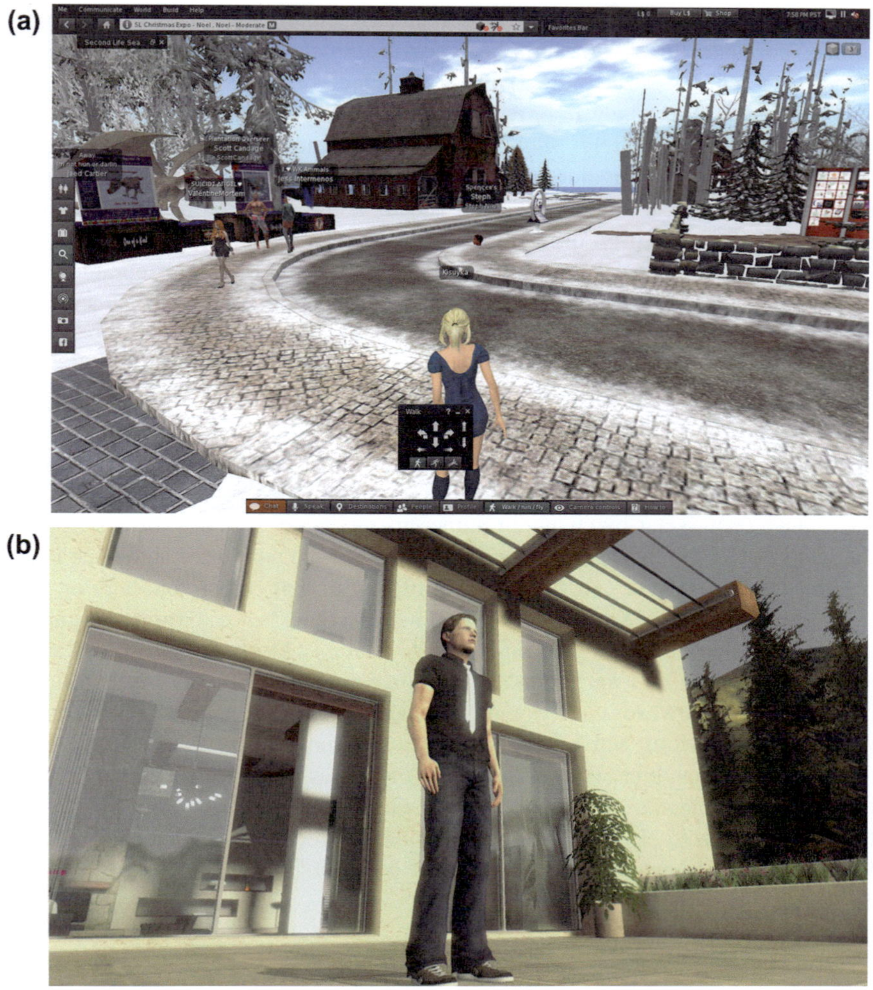

Fig. 5.3 Screenshots of **a** Second Life and **b** PlayStation Home

Second Life had become more interesting than their real life. Indeed, one could put on a body avatar, meet other people without a fear of being rejected, and finally become somebody important and popular, while in real life it could be more challenging to achieve this. However, the regular residents of Second Life were mostly content creators rather than regular Internet browsers. It was easy to arrive there and start walking or flying around, but it required more technical skill to be involved further.

It is possible that this gap between a wish to visit 3D cyberspace and a technical ability to do fully exploit the environment, motivated Google to launch a 3D chat program Lively in 2008, which appeared to be a contained, very simplified version of Second Life. Users of Lively could quickly create their avatars, design 3D rooms, populate them with furniture provided in the online library, and invite friends in to chat. Access to the Lively rooms could be easily embedded into blogs and websites inviting the web browsers to explore another dimension of the web. It has become immediately very popular for those who wanted to talk three-dimensionally by adding to the chat their 3D avatars and virtual environment. However, Google closed Lively at the end of 2008 while the disappointed users attempted to recreate it on different platforms.

The objective to find a reasonable compromise between the complexity of making personal virtual places and the still popular desire to live a second life appeared to motivate Sony Computer Entertainment's London Studio in 2008 to start its own social gaming platform "PlayStation Home" for the PlayStation 3 (PS3) on the PlayStation Network (PSN). Compared to the rather primitive 3D graphics of Lively, PlayStation Home displayed high-resolution images of realistically modeled 3D environments and avatars of the participants supported by the Havok physics engine (Fig. 5.3b). The PS3 owners selected for beta testing could make their own avatar by changing numerous predefined variants, browse through the wardrobe of cloths and accessories, chose a private apartment and stock it with furniture items. At first, everything was provided free of charge, but later on some items became available for a low price, which could be paid from the gamer's account. Of course, the goal of building PlayStation Home was not to sell virtual accessories but to find an alternative way of engaging PS3 users in buying and playing games. However it did not prevent the users walking around, exploring new places, and socializing with other visitors. It was even possible to use a microphone to speak rather than type words. The whole place was a technological breakthrough in terms of immersion, while not giving the same freedom as in Second Life. However, as with Lively, Sony Computer Entertainment decided to close PlayStation Home, which was done in 2015 worldwide, generating disappointment on the part of the PlayStation owners.

5.6 Back to Reality

The Virtual Campus of NTU and Google's StreetView—a technology featured in Google Maps and Google Earth that provides panoramic views from positions along many streets in the world—may be compared in Fig. 5.4. StreetView was launched in 2007 in several cities in the United States, and has since expanded to include cities and rural areas worldwide. A picture is worth a thousand words, but a real picture is worth a thousand simulated images. StreetView has immediately engaged every computer and mobile device user into the experiences which had been previously available only to rather advanced users. Though not really 3D, it delivered the necessary experience of being there. The next step was to add virtual environments to the real-world data. Google produced 3D models of some of the very large cities in the world as well as licenses of SketchUp. Initially offered to the

Fig. 5.4 Screenshots of **a** Virtual Campus of NTU and **b** Google StreetView of the same place

Google users with a goal to make their own 3D models to augment them to Google Maps, SketchUp is a 3D modeling computer program for a wide range of drawing applications such as architectural, interior design, landscape architecture, civil and mechanical engineering, film, and video game design. It is available in a number of versions including a freeware version.

A variety of mobile augmented reality applications followed, and they have brought an additional modality in common human–computer interaction—actual walking. While in SketchUp and other similar aps, we may see the visual image combined from real and simulated images, and with mobile devices using GPS we see how the images are changing depending on our actual location and orientation. We can now ask for a help of the AR-equipped navigator, which shows us how to move from one place to another by actually drawing our way across the constantly changing video image captured by the mobile phone.

The recent explosive popularity of Pokémon Go is one good example of how mixing modes can achieve new dimensions of experience. Instantly VR/AR technologies managed to engage people for whom working with ATM machine was the most challenging computing task so far. In Singapore, practically everyone, regardless of age, began catching pokémons with their mobile phones—fictional interactive 3D characters displayed over real environments, as seen by mobile phone cameras. Many shops and restaurants began "luring" pokémons to attract potential customers to their premises. In addition, the game makers came up with a supporting game legend by saying that it is healthy to play this game because it requires actual walking to reach the goals of the game. Ironically, some people started to translate the goals of the game back to reality and Bintan Island[5] in Indonesia became famous for being a place where one can easily capture Pikachu.[6]

5.7 Lessons Learned

Academia was very much involved in building and using virtual shared spaces. The first most notable involvement was done in populating Active Worlds Educational Universe (AWEDU) with virtual campuses of many universities. Then, Second Life gave another stimulus for electronic education in cyberspace and almost every university created their Second Life representation. Two approaches were explored by the educators: creating virtual replicas of the real educational facilities, and making virtual simulations of the places which do not exist or are costly to generate for educational institutions. The first approach was useful initially because one could enter a virtual classroom and listen to a lecture, or participate in a group class. However, it was soon realized that real-world education facilities are not necessarily appropriate for direct copying into a virtual world. Therefore, a mixture of real and virtual teaching facilities may be more effective. After taking a virtual class

[5]Bintan Island is an island in the Riau archipelago of Indonesia. For some reason Pikachu pokémon, which is very rare in other parts of the world, can easily be spotted and captured near Nirwana Resort Hotel and Bintan Ferry Terminal, as reported by the author's niece Lidia who managed to capture three Pikachus in one day at this location.

[6]Pikachu is a fictional creature that appears in many video games. It is one of the most sought after poket monsters (pokémons) in the Pokémon Go mobile game.

involving a slide presentation, the learners can explore what it looks like to be captured by a virtual hurricane, or a waterfall, or to walk on the lava flow.

However, shared virtual worlds were not equally popular in every context. Some students prefer common text chat rather than 3D immersion. There can be different explanations for this, and, therefore, as in case of VR in general, education in shared virtual spaces has to be optional for those who are not comfortable browsing 3D information online.

On the other hand, mixing realities may be a very promising direction for education since it displays a familiar world and adds 3D interactive helpers to it which are easy to control. Also, the overhead of the time needed to implement 3D VR may become prohibitive for problems which require quick and efficient solutions. Using real images and videos and augmenting these with 3D interactive objects, as well as potentially adding new modalities such as the ability to touch the displayed scenes as if they were the actual 3D scenes, may increase the dimensions of electronic education in cyberspace.

Summary of the Hot Links to Embedded URLs in This Chapter

Section 5.2

Google Glass
https://developers.google.com/glass/
Leap Motion
https://www.leapmotion.com/product/vr

Section 5.3

"The Lawnmover Man"
http://www.imdb.com/title/tt0104692/
"The Thirteenth Floor"
http://www.imdb.com/title/tt0139809/?ref_=fn_al_tt_1
The Matrix
http://www.imdb.com/title/tt0133093/
Divergent
http://www.imdb.com/title/tt1840309/?ref_=nv_sr_1
Minority Report
http://www.imdb.com/title/tt0181689/?ref_=fn_al_tt_1
Microsoft Kinect
http://www.xbox.com/en-US/xbox-one/accessories/kinect
https://developer.microsoft.com/en-us/windows/kinect
Leap Motion
https://www.leapmotion.com/product/vr
Iron Man

http://www.imdb.com/title/tt0371746/?ref_=fn_al_tt_9
Kingsman: The Secret Service
http://www.imdb.com/title/tt2802144/?ref_=fn_al_tt_1
Oculus Rift
https://www.oculus.com/
Sony Virtual Reality Headset,
https://www.playstation.com/en-us/explore/playstation-vr/
HoloLens
https://www.microsoft.com/microsoft-hololens/en-us
Avatar
http://www.imdb.com/title/tt0499549/?ref_=fn_al_tt_1

Section 5.4

Quantum Link
http://www.qlinklives.org/
Commodore 64
http://www.commodore.ca/commodore-products/commodore-64-the-best-selling-computer-in-history/
Lucasfilm
http://lucasfilm.com/
Active Worlds
https://www.activeworlds.com/web/index.php
hope
http://joey1058.blogspot.co.uk/2012/02/cybertowncom-1995-2012-rip.html
visiting,
http://www3.ntu.edu.sg/home/assourin/VirCampus.html

Section 5.5

Habbo
https://www.habbo.com/
There
https://www.prod.there.com/
Second Life
http://secondlife.com/
Entropia Universe
http://www.entropiauniverse.com/
Meez,
https://www.meez.com/
World of Kaneva
http://world-of-kaneva.software.informer.com/4.0/
Ultima Online
http://uo.com/
EverQuest
https://www.everquest.com/register

World of Warcraft
https://worldofwarcraft.com/en-gb/
MapleStory
http://www.maplesea.com/
Phantasy Star Online
http://www.pso2.com/us/ Guild Wars
https://www.guildwars2.com/en/
Disney Club Penguin
http://www.clubpenguin.com/
Whyville
http://www.whyville.net/smmk/nice
Webkinz
http://www.webkinz.com/
Mokitown
http://mokitown.myminicity.com/
Second Life
http://secondlife.com/
closed Lively
https://googleblog.blogspot.co.uk/2008/11/lively-no-more.html
Sony Computer Entertainment
http://www.worldwidestudios.net/locations/europe/london-studio
Havok
https://www.havok.com/

Section 5.6

SketchUp
http://www.sketchup.com/
Pokémon Go
http://www.pokemongo.com/

Further Reading

Brutzman, D., Daly, L.: X3D: Extensible 3D Graphics for Web Authors, p. 470. Morgan Kaufmann Publishers, Burlington, MA. ISBN-13: 0-12-088500-X (2007)

Sourin, A.: Computer Graphics: From a Small Formula to Cyberworlds, 3rd edition, p. 370. Prentice Hall, Singapore. ISBN: 978-981-06-9234-6 (2012)

References

1. Gibson, W.: Neuromancer. Ace, New York City, NY. ISBN: 0-441-56956-0 (1984)
2. Stephenson, N.: Snow Crash. Bantam Books, New York City, NY. ISBN: 0-553-08853-X (1992)
3. Vinge, V.: True Names. Dell Publishing, New York City, NY. ISBN 0-440-10757-1 (1981)

4. Lukyanenko, S.: Labyrinth of Reflections. Amazon Media, ASIN: B01G5XNN90
5. Parisi, A.: Learning Virtual Reality: Developing Immersive Experiences and Applications for Desktop, Web, and Mobile, p. 166. O'Reilly Media, Sebastopol, CA (2015)
6. Nite, S.: Virtual Reality Insider: Guidebook for the VR Industry, p. 192. New Dimension Entertainment (2014)
7. Jerald, J.: The VR Book: Human-Centered Design for Virtual Reality, p. 475. ACM Books, New York (2015)
8. Linowes, J.: Unity Virtual Reality Projects, p. 286. Packt Publishing, Birmingham, UK (2015)
9. http://www.vrs.org.uk/virtual-reality-applications/
10. http://www.virtualaviation.co.uk/flight-simulator-experiences/
11. Schmalsteig, D., Hollerer, T.: Augmented Reality: Theory and Practice (Game Design/Usability), p. 528. Addison Wesley, Boston, MA (2016)
12. Aukstakalnis, S.: Practical Augmented Reality: A Guide to the Technologies, Applications and Human Factors for Ar and Vr (Usability), p. 500. Addison Wesley, Boston, MA (2016)
13. Sourin, A.: Nanyang technological university virtual campus. IEEE Comput. Graph. Appl. **24** (6), 6–8 (2004)

Chapter 6
Case Study: Digital Holography as a Creative Medium to Display and Reinterpret Museum Artifacts, Applied to Chinese Porcelain Masterpieces

Shuo Wang, Ardeshir Osanlou and Peter S. Excell

Abstract Synergies between art and science are explored in a specific context of using digital holograms to represent and contextualize certain great works of Chinese art: Yuan blue-and-white porcelain artifacts. The specific aim of the work was to explore digital holographic printing as an innovative technology to recover detailed comprehensive impressions of cultural relics and their surroundings and environment, as well as to represent historical culture. In addition, digital holographic printing was investigated as a medium for creative display of museum objects, especially those that are too delicate and valuable to be removed from existing cabinets, and to activate viewers' perceptions and to expand their knowledge of archaeological, historical, artistic, and cultural artifacts, all apprehended in the contexts of both their original environment and that in which they were later discovered. A new methodology involving redefinition, recreation, reconstruction, and representation (the "4RE" method) is proposed and applied to achieve these objectives. A new artistic form "Holomontage" was developed as a modality for creative display of museum objects. The proposed technique was successfully applied to an art work portraying the archaeological excavation scene of the site where the largest quantity of Yuan blue-and-white porcelain has been found. The new display methodology "4RE" provides appropriate guidance on optimum usage of the power of holography. This can be argued to be a new creative art form in its own right, which is providing new perceptions for audiences.

Keywords Archaeology · Chinese porcelain masterpieces · Digital holography · Digital holographic printing · Holography · Holomontage · Museology · Museum artifact display · Reconstruction archaeology · Science and art interdisciplinarity · Yuan blue-and-white porcelain

R. Earnshaw, *Research and Development in the Academy, Creative Industries and Applications*, SpringerBriefs in Computer Science,
DOI 10.1007/978-3-319-54081-8_6

6.1 Museology, Museums, and the Potential for New Display Technologies

Museology may be regarded as consisting of cultural studies and cultural theory, with the aim of defining new possibilities and methodologies for curation of artworks, collections, and exhibitions, and their display. The function of a museum can be divided into four aspects: education; preservation (including acquisition); conservation and collection management; and research and communication, which includes education and the staging of exhibitions. Museums are considered to be significant spaces to protect and display both tangible and intangible historical heritage, which is associated with the inventiveness and vitality of human beings. With guidance from developing museology, display plays a vital role in delivering information to the public. Today, virtually all museums focus on the aspect of public service and education, thus audience-oriented research has become essential to assist in satisfying the increasing pressure from both within and outside museums to create effective educational institutions for the general public [1].

As Mae Jemison suggested [2], "*The arts and sciences are avatars of human creativity—they are our attempt as humans to build an understanding of the world around us*." These two disciplines cover a large part of the diverse and wide-ranging interests relating to human activity, but share the same underlying concept of improving human understanding and enlarging the experience of the whole world [3]. When referring to the creative display of museum objects, the combination of science and art has the potential to create a new energy which could expand human knowledge via an innovative means of communication and could motivate the perception of the audience, as well as create an enduring memory for the public. According to Hourston-Hanks et al. [4], museums provide consistently engaging, meaningful, and important memorable experiences which broaden the range and outlook of visitors. For instance, in 2014, the theme of International Museum Day was "Museum Collections Make Connections" [5]. The aim of this was to encourage museums to move away from traditional methods of engagement, and to try to find new methods to make museum objects more accessible to their audiences, driven by the imperative that museums today are increasingly expected to entertain the public and respond to their perceived desires, rather than simply telling them what is thought to be good for them to know.

When displaying a museum object, the narration feature that an object holds a significant position, which could be used to present background information to an audience and enable them more comprehensively to understand the object. Hourston-Hanks et al. [4] noted that, "*As a broad currency, narrative can facilitate the collaboration of professionals and the integration of media, and could therefore play an important part in the creation of powerful and embodied museum experiences*." However, current typical display methods for museum objects struggle to accomplish this. In order to compensate for this failing, it is becoming necessary to use different media to enhance display in an innovative way. In order to excite the public's curiosity and interest, artists are paying attention to the creation of new display methods for museum objects, as a way to unlock the creative potential of collections and to create powerful visitor experiences.

For artists, science can provide new and interesting subject matter, as well as offering new technologies, tools, processes, and skills. Therefore, with the development of ultrarealistic holographic imaging [6], the appearance of a hologram can be used to create new media to display museum objects in a lifelike manner. In this way, the public are unable to differentiate what is real and what is not, providing the potential to explore new approaches to museology.

6.2 Digital Holography

As an alternative to traditional approaches to the display of museum objects, a hologram could compensate for the limitations present in various aspects, such as the display location, the displayed objects, the display topic, and the enhancement of audience motivation and stimulation. For example, within the authors' research group, a holographic image of a Bronze Age axe was created and when it was displayed with the original object (Fig. 6.1), audiences could not tell which was the real image [7]. Furthermore, the limitations of opening times and interior space could be overcome, together with other limitations presented, for example, by politics, war, and geology. The constraints of the number of objects, display space, and the precious character of museum objects could also be solved. Similarly, holograms could be used to bridge a display: for instance many museums currently resort to the simple artifice of replacing objects with printed images if they have been borrowed for another exhibition elsewhere, or removed temporarily for restoration. Such images are obviously a very poor substitute for the real thing.

In contrast, the verisimilitude of holographic images is vastly superior to either paper printing or video displays. Holographic displays have the inherent interferometric ability to reproduce the original distribution of light from a given scene. With the spatial structure, the image can be represented to a resolution of less than 1 micron. In comparison, the information content of current high-definition 3D television (despite having a similar number of several million pixels), is far inferior because each holographic pixel (hogel) itself projects several million different images depending on the angle of view. The static information is a factor of some millions of times greater than that of the high-definition static television display.

In addition, due to advances in digital technology, some scientists have explored the application of digital technology in holographic printing, and this has driven its development. Digital holographic prints are composed of a matrix of holographic pixels, also termed holopixels or hogels. Holopixels are created by the interference of red, green, and blue (RGB) lasers in a holographic medium, such as a photopolymer or silver halide film. Digital holographic printing could utilize a holoprinter or digital holographic printing device to produce digital holograms: these are industrial machines that can produce full-color, purely digital, reflection holograms in a repeatable and reliable manner. Figure 6.2 displays the unique digital

Fig. 6.1 The Bronze Age axe (*below*) and its holographic image (*above*)

holographic printer developed at Wrexham Glyndwr University, used to produce the first experimental digital hologram for this project.

A color digital holographic printer includes several components [7], such as the data source, red, green, and blue lasers, a spatial light modulator (SLM), beam-steering optics, and a computer to show the images on the SLM and to control the whole system. The laser-writing scheme utilizes an object and a

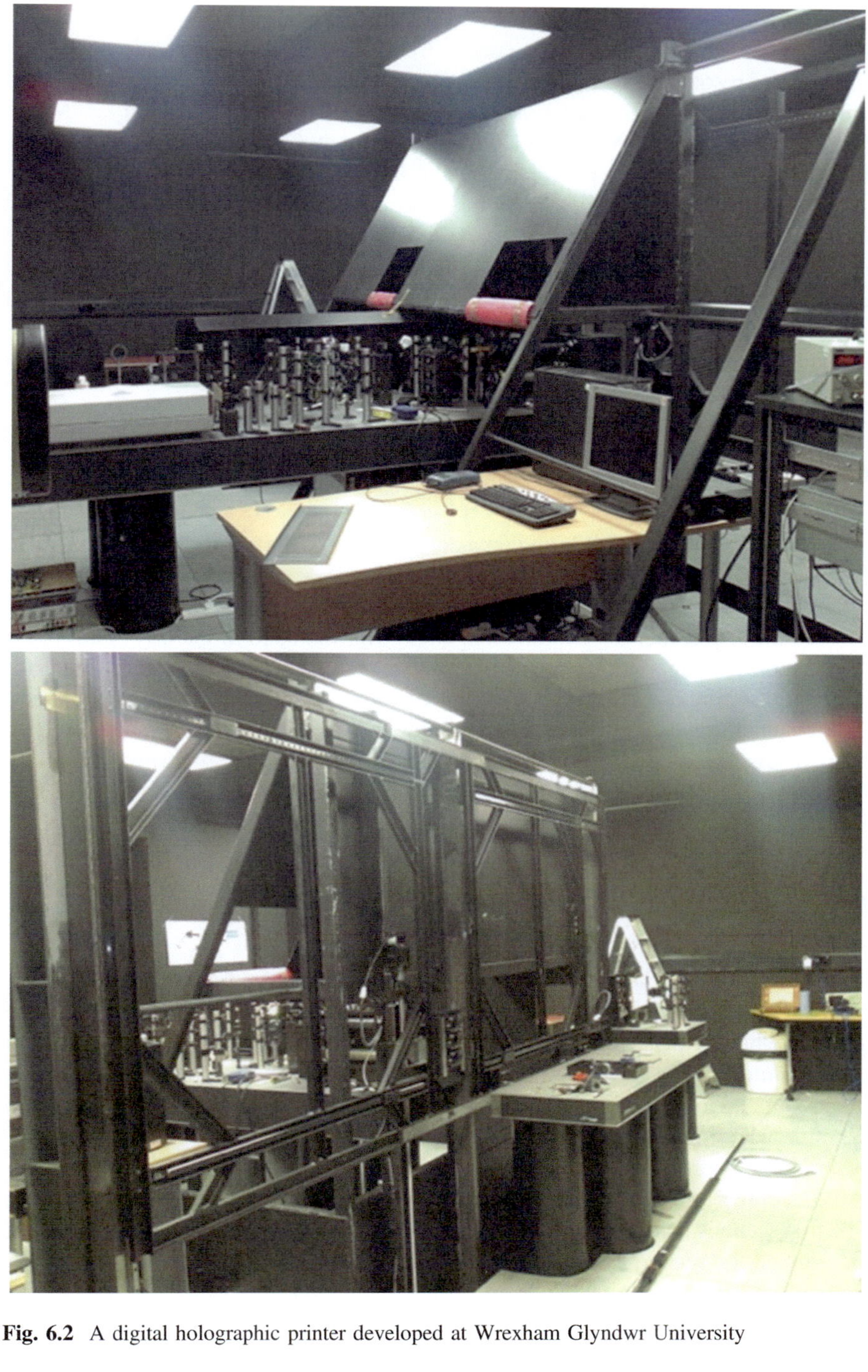

Fig. 6.2 A digital holographic printer developed at Wrexham Glyndwr University

reference beam pair. The object beam is modulated through the SLM using 2D information synthesized from a scene [6]. The data sources should include a selection of resources, such as general artwork and illustrations, photographs taken with cameras, or else digital imagery produced by software such as Maya, SketchUp, 3D Studio Max, AVEVA Review, AutoCAD, Revit, CAD/CAE or CAM files, BIM models, point clouds, and laser scans.

This type of printed digital hologram was utilized to test its usability as a new medium. According to Vergo [8], "*art made with new technology, or to use the more frequent term, 'new media art' is often connected with innovation.*" Hence digital holographic printing which is based on a 3D image possibly combined with modeling via a computer could expand the creativity and add additional background information about an object.

6.3 Holomontage

The term "Holomontage" is based on a combination of the words "holography" and "montage." In broad terms, holomontage refers to a technique which integrates different holographic models or channels into one digital printed hologram. It may involve the application of photomontage and film montage in the creation process of the holomontage, for instance, the montaged 2D pattern could be used for material mapping, as well as the editing method of film montage being applied for a multichannel scene synthesized in a meaningful way. Here, holomontage refers to creative display of museum objects in a synergistic process of recreation of the narration of the object through digital holographic printing.

6.4 The Narrative Construction of Holomontage

The narrative construction of holomontage can be realized in several ways, as follows: flashback, interposed, combined, break, and jumped. Some of them can be used together. A perspective view of a digital printed hologram was simulated in order to interpret the five narrative constructions. The narration of the manufacture process of an iconic item of Chinese porcelain, the Yunlongwen jar, was used as an example which is to be interpreted below.

Figure 6.3 simulates three individual spatial scenes in a horizontal viewing angle of 90°, representing stages in the manufacture of a porcelain artifact of this type. The first scene is from 0 to 30°, which shows the pattern painted on the first firing of the artifact, the second scene is from 30 to 60°, which shows the jar with the glaze applied, and the third scene is from 60 to 90°, which is the final porcelain after firing.

"Flashback narration" refers to a scene in which an earlier scene is inserted into the normal chronological order of a narrative, for instance, if scene A—scene

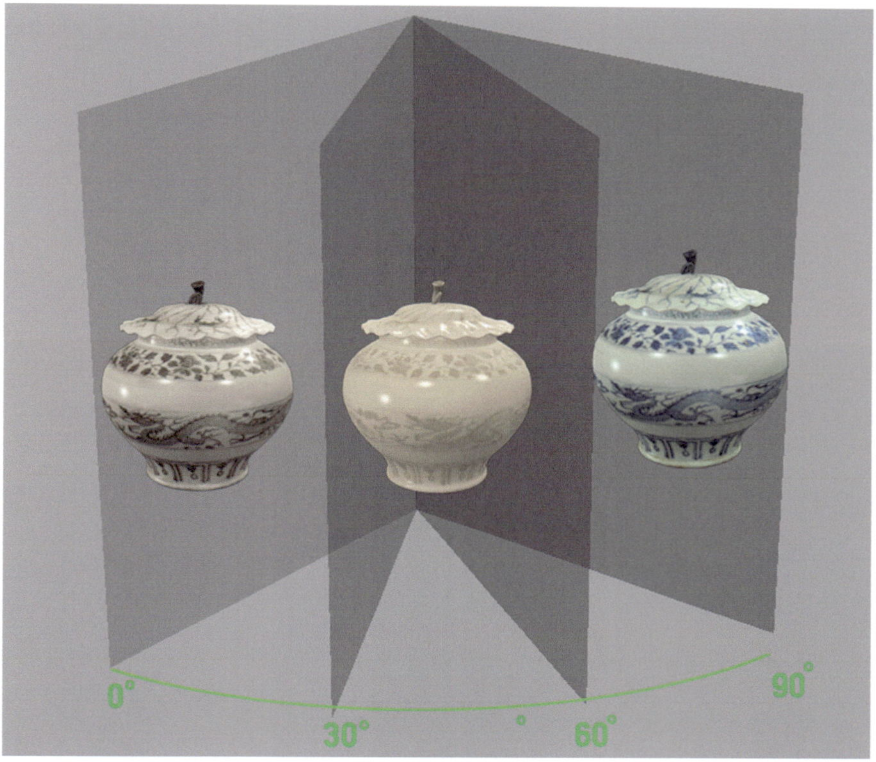

Fig. 6.3 The simulated scene of a digital hologram montage, representing stages in manufacture in this case

B—scene C is the chronological order, then scene B—scene A—scene C or scene B—scene C—scene A will be a flashback order (Fig. 6.4).

"Interposed narration" of holomontage refers to insertion of one or more scenes. For instance, a display containing only two scenes, such as Scene C—Scene B may have another scene interposed, such as: Scene C—Scene A—Scene B (Fig. 6.5).

"Combined narration" in holomontage refers to combining individual scenes together into a new scene. For instance, Scene C + Scene A (Fig. 6.6).

"Break narration" in holomontage refers to separating one spatial scene into partial contributions from two or more scenes. For instance, combining half of each of scenes C and A (Fig. 6.7).

"Jumped narration" in holomontage refers to removing a scene from two or more scenes. For instance, Scene C—Scene A—Scene B having Scene A extracted to become Scene C—Scene B (Fig. 6.8).

Holomontage can not only be seen as a technique for integrated holographic models and channels but also can be seen as a new artistic form for presenting museum objects in a creative way to educate and entertain audiences.

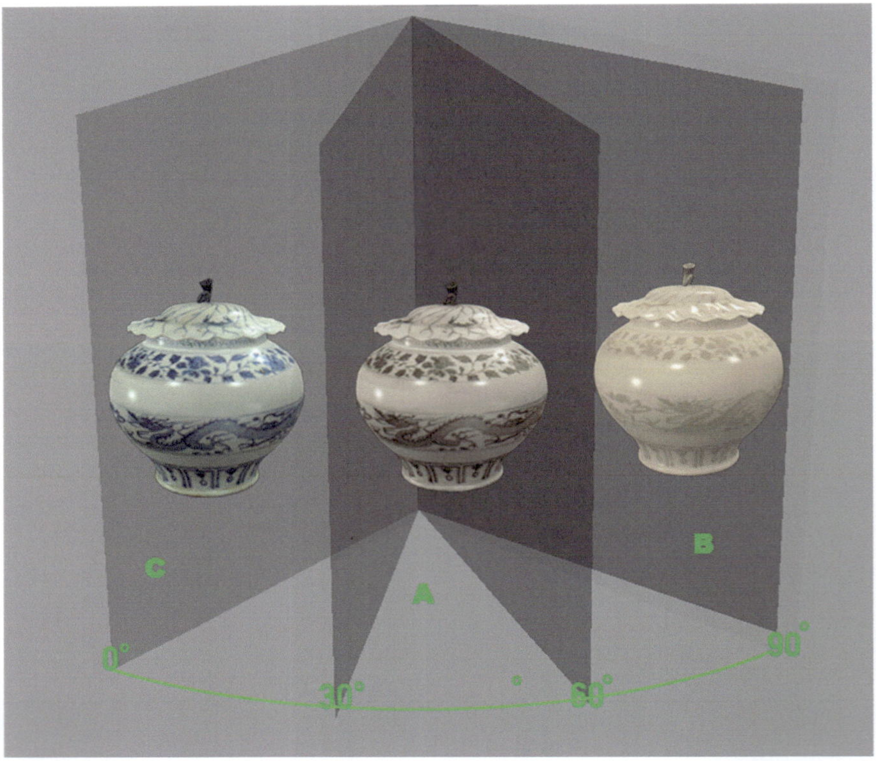

Fig. 6.4 Flashback narration (c.f. Fig. 6.3)

6.5 The Method for Creative Display of Museum Objects

There are various kinds of amorphous problems in the presentation of historical remains or other cultural phenomena that may become common issues in the various stages of the process. Therefore, a comprehensive and appropriate display method, applying the unique features of digital holographic printing, should be propounded and tested to demonstrate resolution of these problems in practice, as well as being applied to the new artistic form of holomontage. These issues resulted in the development of a new platform to address such displays: the "4RE" method.

The "4RE" method covers redefinition, recreation, reconstruction, and representation as the four steps in the implementation of the synergies between an artifact (or conceptually linked group of artifacts) and digital holographic printing. The "4RE" method will be illustrated here in an implementation for an art work of the archaeological excavation scene of the site where the largest quantity of iconic Chinese porcelain (Yuan blue-and-white porcelain) has been excavated.

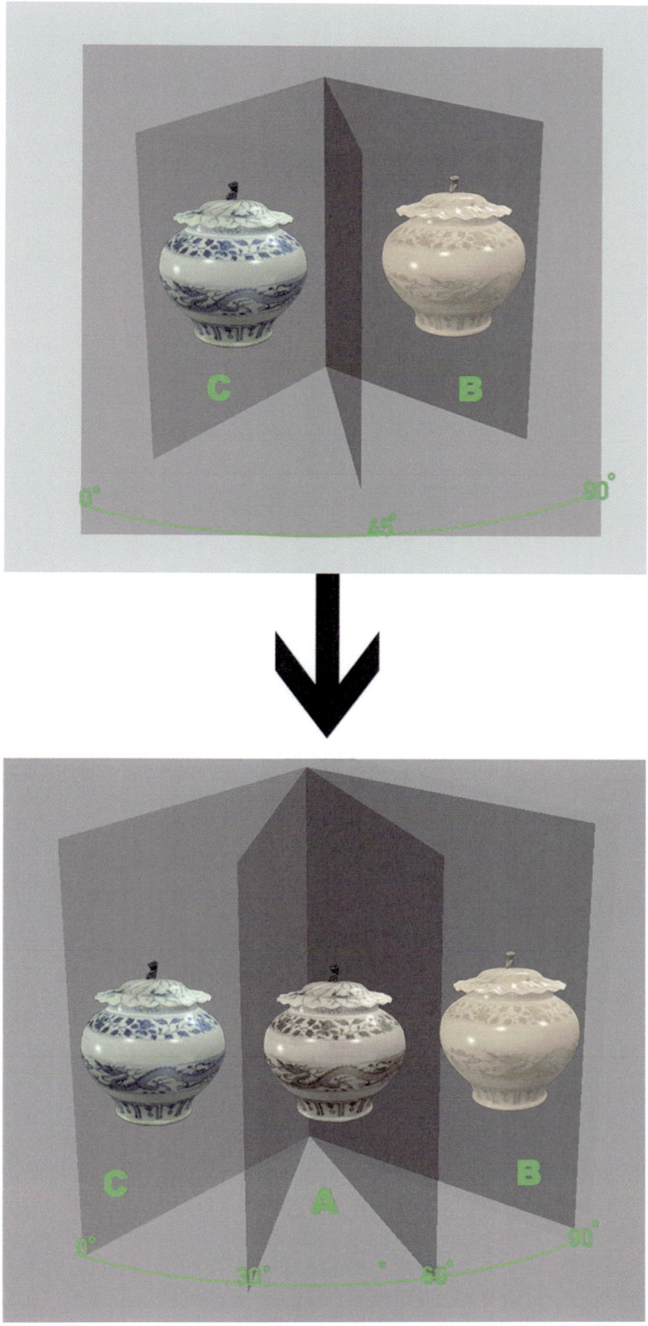

Fig. 6.5 Interposed narration

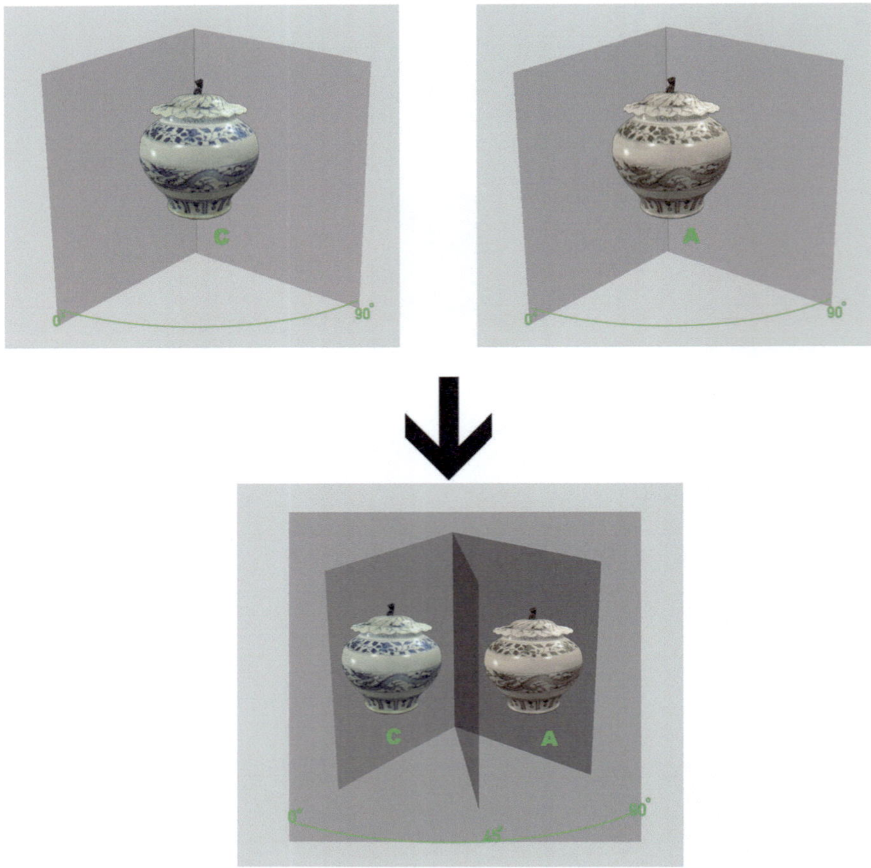

Fig. 6.6 Combined narration

6.6 The Art Work

6.6.1 A Brief Introduction to Yuan Blue-and-White Porcelain

Considering the extensive collection of Chinese cultural relics that exists, there is no doubt that Chinese porcelain enjoys a significant position within the history of Chinese civilization. From the historical remains, it is clear that Chinese porcelain developed over thousands of years, resulting in global connections through trade, and becoming a core aspect of heritage within our world, as well as representing "world art" [9].

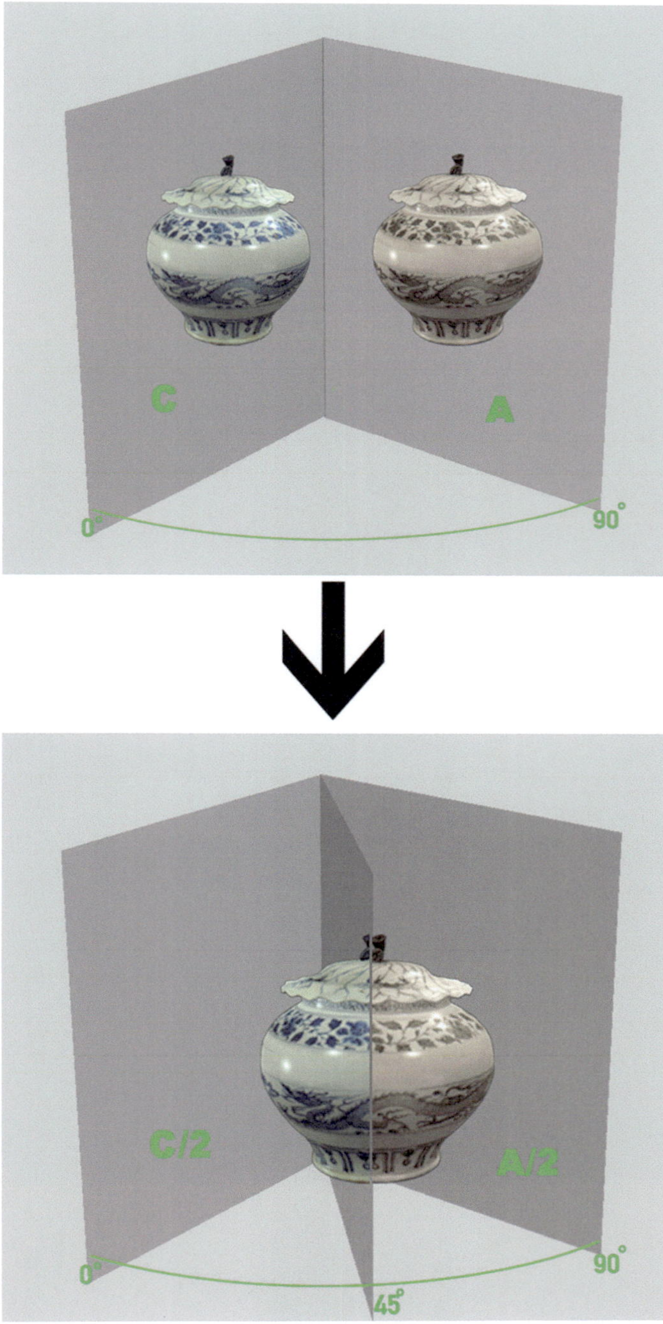

Fig. 6.7 Break narration

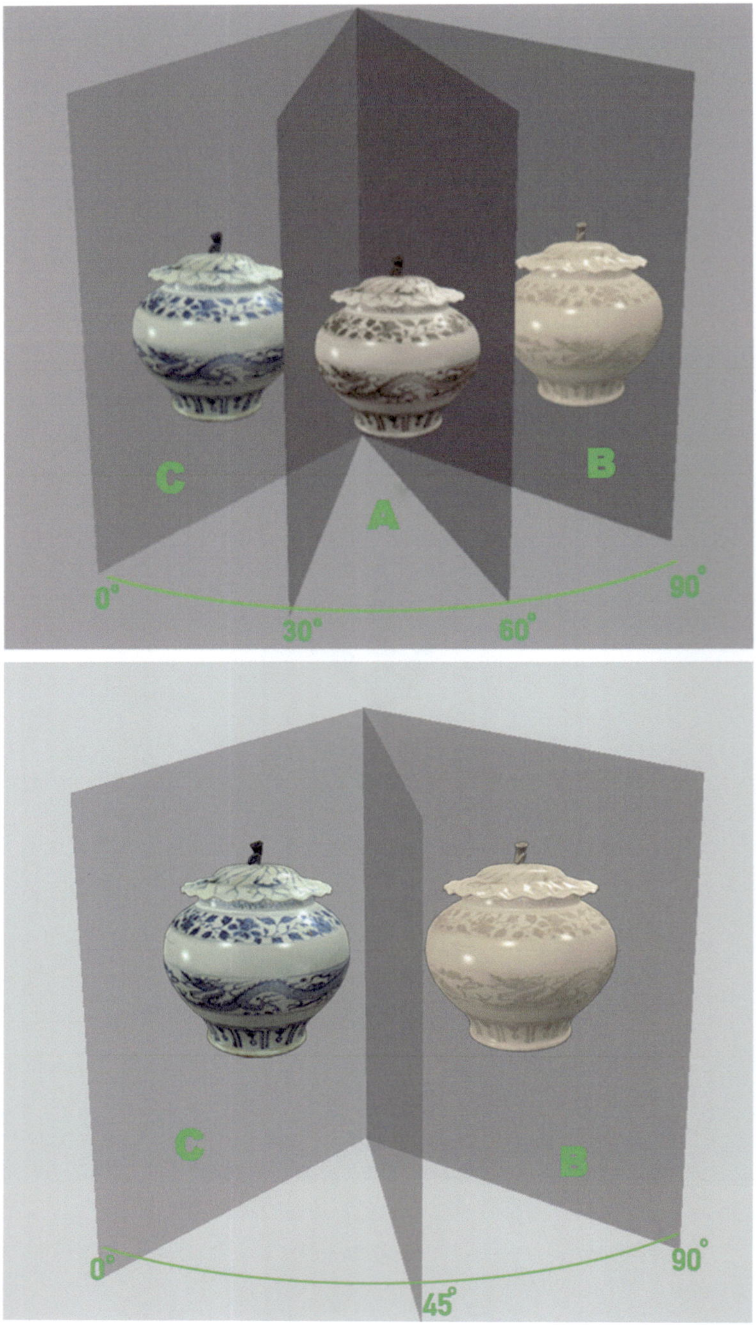

Fig. 6.8 Jumped narration

Yuan blue-and-white (YBW) porcelain is rare, with fewer than four hundred items found across the world. Outside of China, YBW porcelain has mainly been found in Turkey, Britain, Japan, and Iran [9]. Hence, exploring the context of this porcelain in terms of time and space possesses essential meaning in the development of world civilization. Therefore, YBW porcelain will be utilized as an outstanding example to discuss and explore the creative display of museum objects.

As a transitional period in Chinese porcelain production, the Yuan Dynasty (1271–1368 AD) not only played a role in inheriting the past and ushering in the future, but also showed innovations and developments in many aspects. Yuan blue-and-white (YBW) porcelain enjoys major significance, and the YBW porcelain artifacts which were excavated from a cellar in Jiangxi contain multiple important meanings. The archaeological activity that occurred in 1980 resulted in the excavation of the largest quantity of YBW porcelain that has so far been found anywhere in the world. Besides, the YBW porcelain in the cellar was found to be largely intact, which is also a rarity in the experience of international archaeological activity, as well as leaving a profound effect and influence in historical and cultural aspects.

6.6.2 Background Information on the Porcelain Excavation

As recorded by the excavation report, the cellar had a round shape, and was neat inside. The diameter of the cellar was about 1.3 m, and the depth was around 0.8 m. A batch of porcelains and a small amount of bronzes had been stacked neatly, classified into bottles, jars, plates, and bowls that were placed overlapped, the small objects being put inside the larger objects. The top of the cellar had been covered with a metal sheet, which had been heavily corroded by nature. The excavated objects totalled 245 pieces, including four pieces of bronze, two pieces of broken iron, and 239 pieces of porcelain. These porcelain artifacts, which were manufactured in different kilns, included: 168 pieces of Longquan celadon made in the Longquan Kiln, 3 pieces of Jun Porcelain made in the Jun Kiln, a piece of blue vase that was made in the Cizhou Kiln, and 67 pieces of Porcelain made in the Jingdezhen Kiln, especially the 19 pieces of Yuan blue-and-white Porcelain.

The 19 YBW masterpieces included a blue-and-white covered jar with a design of dragons and clouds (Fig. 6.9), two blue-and-white jars with dragons amid clouds, and a lotus leaf shaped cover (Fig. 6.10), as well as further vases, jars, and cups.

Even though the archaeological report of this excavation recorded valuable information about the location and condition of the cellar, as well as the number and as-found position of each porcelain, the information was still not sufficient for digital holographic cultural representation.

Fig. 6.9 A blue-and-white covered jar with a design of dragons and clouds

Fig. 6.10 Two pieces of blue-and-white porcelain with designs of dragons and clouds and a lotus leaf shaped cover

6.6.3 The Creative Process

6.6.3.1 Redefinition

According to the "4RE" method, redefinition is the first as well as the most crucial step, offering the fundamental basis to direct the other steps. Therefore, the content of the redefinition should be analyzed in detail in terms of the artwork creation.

In this work, redefinition commences with identification of the target of this artwork, trying to recover the cellar excavation scene within its cultural context, framed by what could be montaged in a hologram. When the target had been settled, the contents of the redefinition could be provided on the basis of the background information on the archaeological activity, so the related literature documents, archaeological reports, and other resources, as well as the testimonies of the archaeologists, historians, geographers, and other experts who participated in or witnessed the excavation could be involved in the process of accumulating resources to underpin creation of the artwork. The objective in this was to use the novel medium to project the achievements of the past, motivating the audience's interests with this new form, enhancing their knowledge and enriching their perceptions.

When referring to the cellar excavation space in 1980, the record mainly discussed the internal and external space in the cellar, and it will be more appropriate at the present time to explore the inside space through surmises about the external space and from the excavation of the internal space. From this, the totality of the space and any hidden spaces may be explored in a better way.

6.6.3.2 Recreation

In terms of content, recreation is mainly focused on recreating the geographical location of the excavation site, and the replicated placing of 239 pieces of excavated objects, especially the 19 pieces of YBW porcelain in the cellar; in addition the different locations among these cultural relics were significant.

In order to recreate the exact location of the porcelain in the cellar, the related literature resources were first sought, in particular the archaeological report of the excavation activity. The archaeological report clearly recorded the size of the cellar, and the number of cultural relics, however, the specific details about the cellar's environment, the natural lighting, the humidity, and the exact position of the objects were not given in the report. Thus the author contacted several archaeologists, historians, geographers, and other experts who participated in or witnessed the excavation. With the help of the current curator of Gaoan Museum, contact was made with Wu Pingsheng, who was the vice-curator at that time and participated in and witnessed the excavation process: careful efforts were made to help Wu Pingsheng to recall his memory of the excavation that had been dismissed to the back of his mind for more than 30 years. According to his recollections, the weather, the environment, and the positions of the cultural relics at that period have been revived, step by step.

After this, the literature information and the multi-angle pictures of the YBW porcelain provided by the present curator of Gaoan Museum, and Mr. Wu's memory were all gathered together to summarize the narrative features of the excavation. These constitute the four ordered spaces that may be summarized as burial space, condition space, excavation space, and the depth excavation space: these four spaces will be integrated and presented in one digital hologram.

6.6.3.3 Reconstruction

From Wu Pingsheng's perspective, the four sequenced spaces were constructed in 3D software, based on modeling, texturing, lighting, and rendering. Figure 6.11 shows them with a textured effect.

According to the summary in the recreation step, the first space is the burial space, mainly presented through the metal plate that covered the cellar. Lifting the covering metal plate was the way to reveal the mystery of the cellar and to enter the world of the Yuan blue-and-white porcelain. Then, the condition space of the YBW porcelain in the cellar was the second space (Fig. 6.12), and equally the state space of digging. Through the memory of curator Wu, the depth of the burial and the detritus on the surfaces of the objects could be restored. The third space (Fig. 6.13) is the excavation space of the YBW porcelain, mainly focusing on the 3D

Fig. 6.11 A view of the simulated YBW porcelains with texturing in Maya

Fig. 6.12 The simulated condition space of the Yuan blue-and-white porcelain in the cellar (the second space)

Fig. 6.13 The simulated excavation space (the third space)

restoration of each object that was based on the images and data, as provided by Gaoan Museum. The last space (Fig. 6.14) is the artifact interior space. According to the literature information and curator Wu's memory, it was possible to restore the disposition of several small objects that were hidden in the large objects, especially the nine stemmed cups that had been laid in the large jar, apparently as a careful act of storage, thus supporting the intensive study of the ancient burial methods and habits in China (presuming that the burial was ancient).

6.6.3.4 Representation

Based on the recovered information, the data for each space has been collected, optimized, and reconstructed in 3D software, so that the database of each space was established sufficiently to print. Next, the four spaces were generated into one

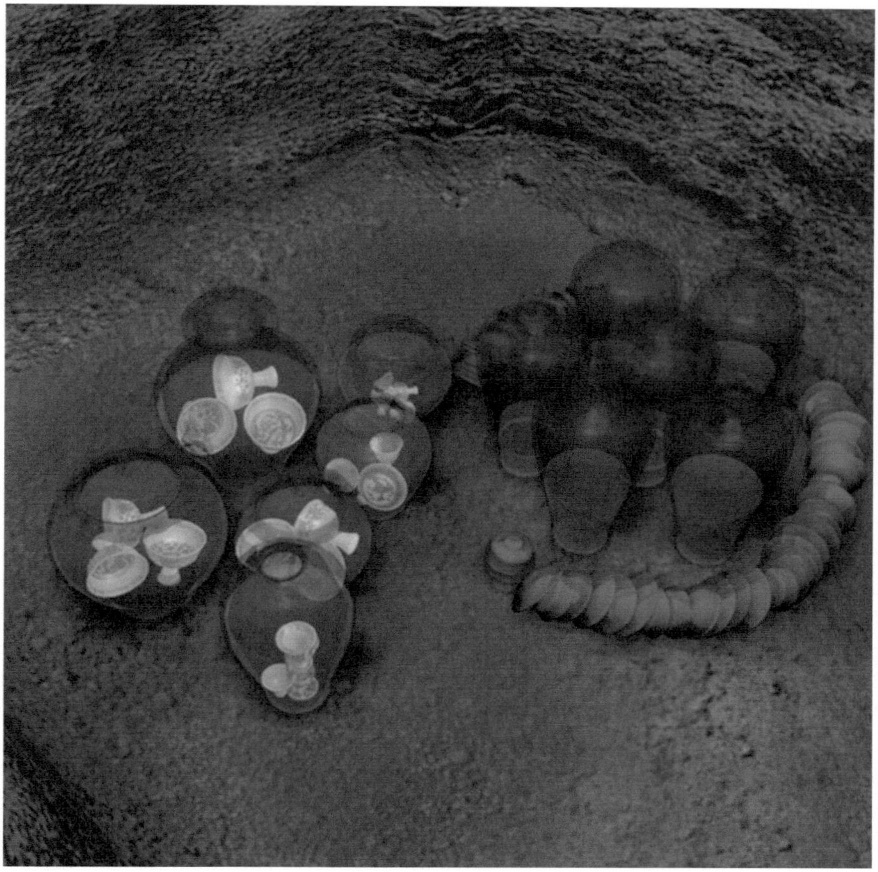

Fig. 6.14 The artifact interior excavation space (the fourth space)

digital hologram and printed by the Zebra Imaging Company [10]. As the hologram is rotated, it may be observed either in clockwise or anticlockwise directions, offering two different viewing experiences to the audience (Fig. 6.15). The clockwise narration was on the basis of the memory of curator Wu, in other words, it can be regarded as the excavation process of these artworks; conversely, the anticlockwise view could present the narrative process of the owner who buried these porcelains in the historical period. Therefore, this digital hologram could not only recover the excavation scene of the YBW porcelain, but also provide the "cultural representation" of two alternative narratives to the audience with this new creative display method.

In this artwork, the digital hologram, as an innovative medium, not only enables the viewer to recover the cellar excavation space in 1980, and to make a sequential spatial visualization of it, but also the loss of information owing to the restricted conditions at that time could be bridged, bringing a profound influence upon

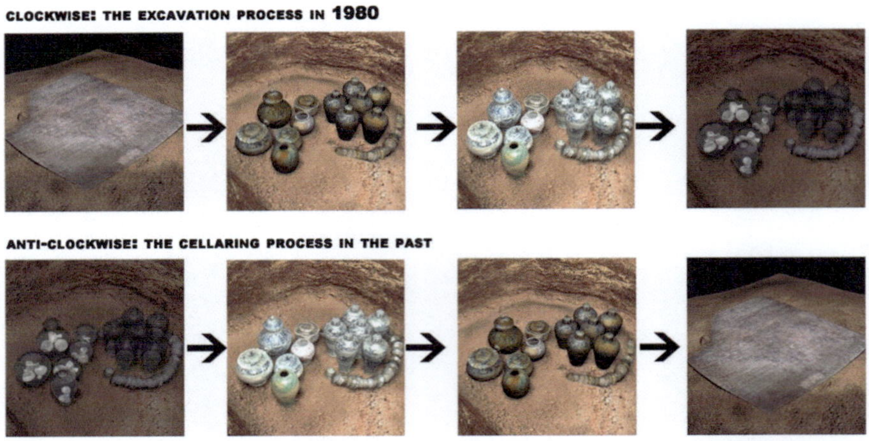

Fig. 6.15 Two ways of viewing the hologram

archaeological, historical, geological, and artistic representation of recovered cultural relics. Furthermore, the final artwork is an artistic form that reveals the diverse features of holomontage that combine with the creativity and technology in this process.

This holographic artwork has been exhibited in central Beijing in 2016. In order to build a more realistic effect for the audience, some extra environments were created; specifically, a surround of artificial soil (Fig. 6.16), some typical working men's shoes, an appropriate illumination system including a bulb and a coal-oil type of lamp chimney, treatment of the floor, including several individual warning lines with the words "no digging" printed on them, and a large LED screen showing the people who undertook the archaeology in 1980. This holographic artwork installation maximized the perception of the excavation as well as facilitating reinterpretation of the current worldview for the audience. The public reaction to the display was very positive and demonstrated the potential of this type of technology in artistic and hybrid artistic-factual displays.

6.7 Lessons Learned

The benefits of the project included the following:

1. To enable much better artificial displays in museums, recreating missing artifacts and missing work scenes through the use of synthetic holograms.
2. To use synthetic holograms as a creative art form: this is briefly summarized in the creative reconstruction of the excavation scene, but the potential is there to create more radical imagery.

Fig. 6.16 The artificial soil surrounding the hologram

3. The technique was satisfactory for general display purposes. The best resolution (better than one micron) is achieved with analogue holography: digital holography still has visible pixelation but an equivalent resolution of 0.5 mm viewed at one meter is considered adequate. In principle, better resolution can be overcome with more powerful computers and printers with higher resolution, but the data quantities become very large and the speed of production of the holograms, already very time-consuming, will become even slower.

4. A major innovation that the team has worked on has been the digital printer. However, this was not aimed at lowering cost or simplification; rather, the objective has been to make much larger hologram prints than previous efforts, thus producing large holographic screens the size of substantial paintings, etc. The increase in size thus effectively lowers the cost per square centimeter. Software to create digital holograms was largely nonexistent before the team commenced its work some years ago, so new software was developed. This should assist future work.

Lessons learned included the following:

1. Non-holographic photographs (e.g., as placed in cabinets when exhibits are temporarily removed for conservation) are much less appealing to exhibition visitors and they fail to give the 3D and realism aspects that are possible with holograms. The key problems to be addressed are the cost and complexity of the hologram-generating equipment.
2. All the current equipment still requires major skill, experience, and adjustment to create a hologram. It is important to understand also that there are two different approaches: to take a hologram "photograph" of an object, an analogue system is used, typically requiring three high-power lasers costing hundreds of thousands of pounds, sitting on an optical bench weighing many tons. The artifacts to be "photographed" have to be brought to the laboratory, although the results are very good, being potentially indistinguishable from the original artifact. The digital method is lighter and requires less powerful lasers, but requires vastly more programming and does not produce such photorealistic outputs. In the project discussed here, the artifacts were too delicate to remove from the museum and so they could not be "photographed" by the analogue method. Instead traditional photographs were taken from a number of angles and then used to recreate the shapes of the objects using solid modeler software which was then used to create the digital holograms. This is very challenging and required very skilled personnel and a number of days to complete the work, culminating in about 6 h to produce one hologram (for the largest, 1 m^2, holograms that can be printed in the state-of-the-art machine shown in Fig. 6.2).
3. In the medium term, it may be possible for the cost to be contained such that it could be offered to the public by bureaux that could be set up in major cities to produce custom products at a reasonable price.
4. Wider use would need lower cost equipment for holographic imaging and for printing of holograms, plus simpler software for creation of digital holograms.
5. The state-of-the-art technology is costly but the pattern of technological evolution suggests that eventually mass production and commoditization could reduce costs. Holography may be compared with what has happened with 3D printing which was previously very costly but is now a commodity product.

6. At this scale of operation, the most likely area for lessons to be learned would be recreation of the archaeological scene and, at minimum, education of inexperienced museum staff in modern views on how to undertake archaeology and not to lose vital evidence that could be overlooked by those not skilled in the art.
7. The techniques could be used for the warriors in the Qin Tombs near Xi'an, but larger and much more expensive and slower equipment would be needed.
8. The use of new technologies is difficult, requiring a long learning period, and is very costly, hence the rate of uptake will be slow. However, this applies to all innovative technologies and technological evolution studies suggest that eventually a commoditization phase appears in which the cost goes down rapidly, the uptake goes up rapidly, and the technology evolves rapidly. Holography, despite having been around for quite a long time, has not yet reached that phase.

6.8 Summary

This chapter has presented an exploration of the synergies between science and art for the creative display and reinterpretation of museum artifacts. The new artistic form "Holomontage" as well its narrative construction has been explored and demonstrated. A new methodology "4RE" which involves redefinition, recreation, reconstruction, and representation, has been successfully applied to the art work of the archaeological excavation scene of the site where the largest quantity of a major type of Chinese cultural artifact (Yuan blue-and-white porcelain) was discovered. The artwork recreating the scene of discovery of the artifacts was successfully tested in a major exhibition.

Acknowledgements The authors gratefully acknowledge the assistance of the following people with the provision of illustrations, which are used with their approval:

Mr. Liu, Curator of Gao'an Museum, and photographer Shang Zhao (Figs. 6.9 and 6.10); Professor Hans Bjelkhagen (Fig. 6.1). All of the other figures are the work of Shuo Wang.

References

1. Greenhill, E.H.: The Educational Role of the Museum. Routledge Press, London and New York (1999)
2. Jemison, M.: Teach Arts and Sciences Together (2009). TED. Available from:www.ted.com/talks/mae_jemison_on_teaching_arts_and_sciences_together/transcript?language=en. Last accessed 04 April 2016
3. Wright, A., Linney, A.: The Art and Science of a Long-term Collaboration. University College London repository. (2006). http://www.ucl.ac.uk/conversation-piece/Wright_Linney%20N_Cpaper.pdf. Last accessed 04 April 2016

4. Hourston-Hanks, L., Hale, J., Macleod, S.: Introduction: Museum Making, the Place of Narrative. In: Hourston-Hanks, L., Hale, J., Macleod, S.: Museum Making. Routledge, Oxford (2012). https://www.scribd.com/doc/231534653/Museum-Meanings-Suzanne-Macleod-Laura-Hourston-Hanks-Jonathan-Hale-Museum-Making-Narratives-Architectures-Exhibitions-Ro
5. International Council of Museums (ICOM). Launch of international museum day 2014—Museum collections make connections (2014). http://icom.museum/press-releases/press-release/article/launch-of-international-museum-day-2014-museum-collections-make-connections/. Last accessed 06 July 2016
6. Bjelkhagen, H., Brotherton-Ratcliffe, D.: Ultra-realistic Imaging: Advanced Techniques in Analogue and Digital Colour Holography. CRC Press, Boca Raton. ISBN: 978-1-4398-2799-4 (2013)
7. Bjelkhagen, H., Cook, J.: Colour holography of the oldest known work of art from Wales. Tech Res Bull British Museum **4**, 88 (2010)
8. Vergo, P.: The New Museology. Reaktion Books Ltd., London (2006)
9. Pierson, S.: The movement of Chinese ceramic appropriation in global history. University of Hawaii Press, J World History **23** (1), 9–39 (2012) (special issue: Global China)
10. Zebra Imaging Inc., Austin Texas, USA. The homepage of Zebra Imaging. http://www.zebraimaging.com/. Last accessed 22 July 2016

Chapter 7
Case Study: Improving the Physical Properties of Materials by Collaboration Between Industry and the Academy

Elvin L. Nix

Abstract This Case Study describes a collaborative scientific research project carried out between Thorn EMI Central Research Laboratories, Hayes, Middlesex, and Leeds University Physics Department in the period 1980–1988. The work brought together two previously unconnected research themes, namely the preparation of highly oriented polymers with improved physical properties, and studies of electrical activity in a special class of polar plastics. Certain common plastics such as polythene may undergo high degrees of molecular orientation during deformation. Leeds University had pioneered the fabrication of high modulus polythene by tensile drawing to create fibres comparable in strength to aluminum. Independently, Thorn EMI had developed a separate class of electrically active plastic materials in various forms for hydrophone and infrared sensor applications. The collaborative work stemmed from the premise that there might be merit in applying the guidelines established for the ultra-orientation of polythene to the electrically active polar plastics, with the specific aim of obtaining materials with improved electrical activity for industrial applications. It was also recognized that such studies would add to the understanding of the complex origins of the electrical activity by creating materials with novel structures. The prospect of elucidating the mechanisms was of considerable scientific interest and complemented existing research interests in the physics department at Leeds. In parallel, the prospect of developing materials with enhanced properties was an attractive goal for Thorn EMI. The basic concept of the collaborative work that high molecular orientation in polar polymers would yield improved electrical responses, had the merit of presentational simplicity, and thus attracted attention and funding. The scientific reality was much more complex, less transparent to the uninitiated, and did not easily match the expectations of those whose interests were primarily commercial. Nevertheless the collaboration was fruitful, resulting in a number of publications for both institutions and in novel products for Thorn EMI. Acquisition of comprehensive data sets on the properties of these novel materials was a very considerable experimental task requiring existing expertise from previous work and specialized equipment at both institutions. The data sets led to a relatively complete description of contrasting materials, permitting precise identification of the dipolar component in each macroscopic electrical response and therefore informed speculation about its origins.

R. Earnshaw, *Research and Development in the Academy, Creative Industries and Applications*, SpringerBriefs in Computer Science,
DOI 10.1007/978-3-319-54081-8_7

Keywords Improved physical properties · High molecular orientation · Joint use of resources · Accelerated timescale · Commercial drive · Risk analysis

7.1 Creating the Collaboration

This collaboration, between a UK industrial research laboratory (part of the Thorn EMI group based in West London) and a UK university (Leeds), was initiated by a clear commercial interest from the industrial partner, and was under the direction of Professor I.M. Ward FRS. The interest was focused on the development of a special class of electroactive plastics for use in a wide range of sensor devices for applications ranging from domestic to military. The general background to the work at Thorn EMI was the application of such specialized plastics to underwater sound detection and infrared sensors [1–4].

A survey of current research interests in UK universities had shown that Leeds had critical expertise in a particular area, namely the fabrication of common plastics with a high degree of molecular orientation by tensile drawing and extrusion [5–8]. These common highly oriented plastics had already exhibited novel properties, such as high tensile strength and high thermal conductivity. The question of whether the same fabrication techniques could be applied to the special class of electrically active plastics (Fig. 7.1), with a view to enhancing their properties and possibly

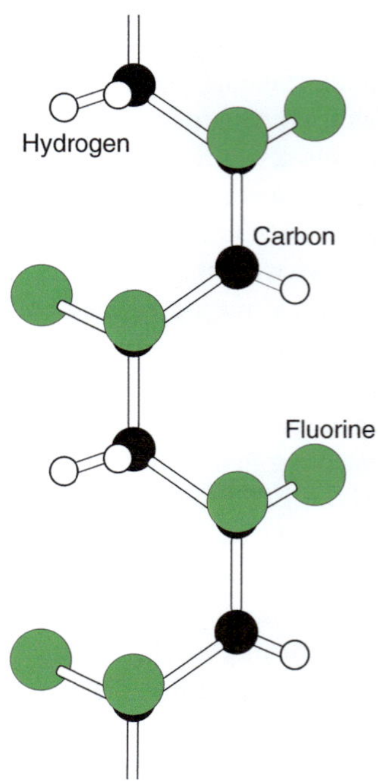

Fig. 7.1 Representation of a common polymorph of polyvinylidene fluoride, the most electrically active plastic

creating novel materials, was addressed in the initial meetings of the proposed collaboration.

Thus there were clear incentives from the outset for both camps in the collaboration. The motivation was both scientific and commercial, with potential benefits for all participants. While the industrial partner had sensitive interests to protect in respect of the marketplace, and confidentiality was a crucial consideration, there were clearly areas of the collective work which could be published in the open literature without compromising these interests. It was thus anticipated that Leeds University would benefit from financial input from the industrial partner, with the creation of academic consultancies, studentships, postdoctoral work and publications. Similarly, it was anticipated that Thorn EMI would benefit greatly from the Leeds knowledge base and the expertise of existing staff. The primary commercial incentive was the creation of new products on an accelerated timescale, but the raised profile of the company in the relevant literature would also be of significant value.

The creation of this collaboration was thus motivated by the urgent need for specialist expertise to be supplied from academia, and encouraged by the application of this expertise to the demand for products in the real world of applications.

7.2 Assessing the Benefits

Clearly, commercial companies and academic institutions have very different objectives. The former exist to create wealth for the shareholders, and the latter to generate scientific publications for the furtherance of knowledge. Can such diverse interests, when pooled, generate positive benefits? The consensus conclusion, based on this collaboration and on similar ones crossing the divide between pure and applied knowledge, is that the benefits are significant when the diversity of interests is managed effectively and participants appropriately incentivized. In this collaboration, several benefits were perceived as key, such as the pooling of resources, the commercial drive and timescale, and the coming together of minds from two worlds. While the objectives of commerce are usually short-term and driven by the demands of the market, this same feature can also be a driving force to energize the more measured pace of academia and accelerate progress.

To give a specific example in respect of physical resources, Thorn EMI needed to produce wide-sheet electroactive plastics rather than the small-scale research fibers and rods fabricated at Leeds. Production of highly oriented wide films and sheets (suitable, for example, for submarine hydrophones) required very large-scale specialized and expensive equipment more appropriately funded at the commercial end of the collaboration. Similarly, electrical polarization of thick plastic sheets required specialized high voltage sources (up to half a million volts). Again, such equipment, with all its essential safety features, was more appropriately operated by the commercial partner. Equally, specialist equipment existing at Leeds, of the kind more suited to academic investigations (such as X-ray crystallography) could be shared by the team at Thorn EMI. This pooling of resources, of equipment, expertise, and experience, proved to be an accelerator of progress, giving both camps access to facilities which they would not ordinarily have had without the need for significant capital spend.

Other perceived benefits were less tangible, but attractive. The meetings of such a collaboration could include an element of blue-sky research not normally countenanced in a strictly commercial setting. Similarly, there would be a pseudo-scientific brainstorming of commercial possibilities in an atmosphere unbridled by the strictures of company routine. Correspondingly, there could be commercial discussion of how to prioritize the scientific research in a manner perhaps foreign to an academic environment. This was perceived as a productive synergy which would act as a focus and driving force for participation at all levels in the sharing of ideas and experience.

7.3 Sustaining the Collaboration

The practical question arose of how to sustain a long-term collaboration between institutions with diverse interests separated by 200 miles. The sustaining tasks were perhaps of two main kinds, involving both technical and political components. As might be expected, there were ongoing tensions between the reality of tortuously slow scientific progress, the fast-moving world of commerce and the need for quick and dependable answers. Scientific rigour must not be sacrificed, but the demand to secure ongoing funding meant that conflicts and compromises were sometimes unavoidable.

First, it was essential to have regular summaries of work in both camps, particularly of those activities which had a direct bearing on funding. These consisted of monthly reports in each area of the collaboration, for both technical and less-technical readers, and less frequent quarterly meetings of key staff. There was an ongoing pressure to demonstrate both short-term goals attained, and to provide a taste of the "promise" of longer term objectives. But the tedious tasks of real research and development often provide results which are difficult to interpret in the short term. In the absence of conclusive data, there arises a political element to the interpretation of the interim data. Inevitably such interpretation is focused at the encouragement of those who control the funding. The risk was that cherry-picked data, used to meet the needs of the moment, had less scientific validity. This was one of the less desirable features of the collaboration, but is perhaps commonplace and unavoidable. Figure 7.2 shows early data of the collaboration which indicated some of the possibilities for enhanced molecular orientation in electroactive plastics.

Second, there was the need to maintain the ongoing interests and incentives of staff who did not have full visibility of the larger project goals. These interests covered a wide range, from consultancy contracts and postdoctoral fellowships to maintaining the ongoing work of students aiming at academic qualifications. For them the endpoint was not so much commercial products as a satisfactory conclusion to the particular part of the work undertaken by them (e.g., Fig. 7.2).

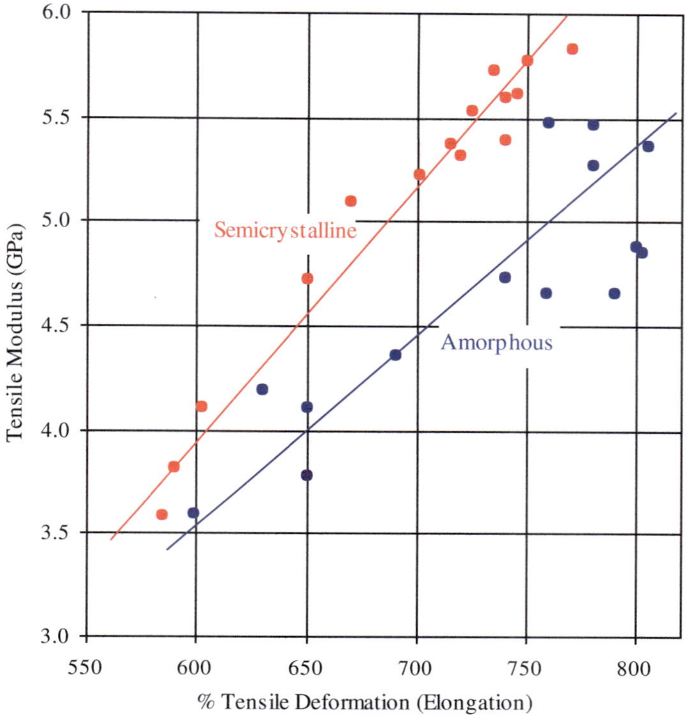

Fig. 7.2 An illustration of the effects of molecular stretching (orientation) on the tensile modulus (stiffness) of fibers of an electrically active plastic poly(vinylidene fluoride). The "semi-crystalline" samples were slowly cooled from the melt whereas the "amorphous" samples were quenched

Obviously some of these needs had a long-term aspect, and were the subject of ongoing anxieties about continuity. To a lesser extent, the university's interest in publications, regardless of whether commercial expectations were met, did not sit comfortably within the commercial thrust.

Managing all these conflicting strands of the project was largely the function of Professor I.M. Ward, FRS, whose prior experience in both the academic and commercial spheres proved indispensable. Thus, we might conclude that the management of multifaceted project of this nature requires a special choice of oversight, without which success is not guaranteed.

7.4 Dependency on Key Participants

As noted above, it was clear from the outset of the collaboration that success depended crucially on scientific input from Leeds University. The prior experience of such joint ventures, on the part of the Chair of the physics department, was critical in respect of his management of the politics of funding, his influence on the commercial partners at Thorn EMI, and his international reputation in the field of polymer research. Without this steadying hand in the picture, it is improbable that the collaboration could have been sustained. Although this was clearly a significant benefit to the project, there could have been significant implications for the project if such a key person had moved to other employment. This dominance, of a single individual, raised concerns about the associated risk from a commercial point of view, which were never addressed.

While the key role was never in question, other individuals participated in coordinating roles which were also central to success. Among these was the commercial head at Thorn EMI, who organized strategy meetings and promoted funding of personnel and capital equipment. He provided an enthusiasm and a selective and optimistic use of scientific data which might have been inappropriate in an academic setting, but which nonetheless added impetus and drive.

Another key component was the role of a Ph.D. student, also employed as a staff-scientist at Thorn EMI, whose function was to provide working input in both camps and to commute regularly between them. This person spent long periods in both locations, and provided an ongoing reporting link for the commercial end. In such an arrangement, of course, the motivation to complete a doctorate was a very useful driving force. It might be claimed that the "voluntary exploitation" of his particular role was also an essential ingredient of continuity and success, and demonstrates very effectively how incentives in general can be an important component of a collaborative exercise.

7.5 Collaboration Locations

To what extent did the physical co-location of the collaborating institutions present an inconvenience or a limiting factor in progress? The physical separation proved an inconvenience in practice, since at that time video conferencing was not commonplace. Return same-day travel was demanding. This had the effect of reducing the frequency of meetings and numbers of participants. Larger meetings, with inclusion of more of the contributors, became rare, a feature partly driven by cost considerations. This lack of wider participation in planning and progress meetings had some drawbacks, particularly on the industrial site where the ongoing aspects of the academic work at Leeds became less visible, less comprehensible and perhaps appeared less relevant. Although the presence of Thorn EMI staff at the University was more frequent than that of Leeds staff at the London end, it was still the case that the academic staff had a limited concept of the ongoing applications work. This communication problem was alleviated to some extent by the frequently commuting Ph.D. student, who provided some of the visibility lacking.

7.6 Collaboration Oversight

Structures for oversight of the collaboration were limited, consisting primarily, but not exclusively, of a department head from each site. Internal controls at Leeds were effective, but it was not obvious how to give Thorn EMI clear visibility of the precise way in which funds were being used by the University. Additionally Leeds appointed an employee to look after the "business interests" of the University, which restricted some freedoms. In general, the arrangements put in place had the merit of simplicity, but the drawback was tunnel vision and a lack of appropriate commercial input. A single research theme tended to dominate the scene, which was perhaps the theme which proved in the end to be of most value to Leeds. It could be summarized as "higher molecular orientation yields larger electrical responses." While this concept had all the attractions of a straightforward presentational slogan for industrial managers appealing for funding, it proved ultimately to be too simple, and ignored the real complexities. Other related research themes could have been considered, but were not. This misplaced focus did not affect the scientific successes, because novel materials gave rise to novel scientific data for publications, but the particular results achieved were of limited commercial value.

Thorn EMI were perhaps more interested in the potential commercial outcomes, than the scientific bases for these outcomes. This may have led to an emphasis on particular aspects of the work at the expense of others, some of which did not lead to a commercial outlet.

7.7 Assessing the End Result

Was the end result of the collaboration worth the effort and money spent? The answer to this question, while broadly affirmative, varied somewhat between the individual participants. From the university's perspective, a range of international publications resulted, indicating substantial scientific progress in the field of ferroelectric behavior of polar polymers. This result was a success for the individual academic participants and in some degree a success also for Thorn EMI, raising the profile of the company in a competitive field. This included published results also from students and staff based at the company [9–16].

From a commercial perspective, however, the results were positive but rather short-lived. A changing market place, and competition from other sources, made some products quickly obsolete. For example, the US Navy market for submarine hydrophones was lost soon after the collaboration finished. Obviously, this particular customer had invested heavily in their area of need, rapidly created competitive products and did not wish to be dependent on a UK supplier.

In contrast, from an academic point of view, the acquisition of comprehensive data sets on these novel materials led to a relatively complete scientific description and elucidation of the origins of the responses. The generation of such data was a gigantic experimental task requiring sustained effort of a type which does not generate headlines, or is necessarily welcomed in a commercial environment. In such complex undertakings a point is reached where only those deeply involved in the research can see the end to which it pointing.

7.8 Lessons Learned

A wide range of staff contributed to the collaboration from both institutions. At Leeds these included the head of the Physics Department, senior lecturers, a number of postdoctoral workers and Ph.D. students. In this diffuse environment it was occasionally difficult to discern where the precise project boundaries lay because of overlap of interests. At Thorn EMI about a dozen persons of varying seniority contributed to the project over a period of about ten years. These included the head of department, administrative, scientific and engineering personnel, the latter because some heavy equipment design and construction was involved. As already mentioned, one of the scientific staff undertook Ph.D. studies during the project, commuting frequently between Leeds and London, being partly resident in both locations and providing regular communication between the two sites. This ensured frequent reporting in both scientific and practical matters, but its effectiveness depended strongly on the incentive to acquire experimental data for a doctorate.

Lessons learned included the following:

1. Looking back at the complex mix of project personnel and the forces driving them, it could be concluded that there should have been a clearer identification from the outset of all the participants, their precise functions and potential contributions, particularly from the commercial point of view.
2. Involvement of more of the contributors in planning and progress meetings would have generated an awareness of the wider picture into which their part fitted. The tendency was smaller meetings of controlling staff, with poor dissemination of information to the project fringes.
3. The communication improvements could have included a better presentation of the basic science to those at Thorn EMI controlling the level of commercial input. Over simplified research themes let to a misplaced emphasis on particular investigations at the expense of other themes which might have been more productive.
4. Obviously some of the needs of the work had a long-term aspect, and were the subject of ongoing anxieties about continuity. To a lesser extent, the university's interest in publications, regardless of whether commercial expectations were met, did not sit comfortably within the commercial thrust.
5. While "higher molecular orientation yields larger electrical responses" was a concept which had all the attractions of a straightforward presentational slogan for industrial managers appealing for funding, it proved ultimately to be too simple, and ignored the real complexities. Other related research themes could have been considered, but were not.

6. Inevitably, funding was allocated by senior persons with incomplete scientific understanding. A better presentation of the fundamental science at this level could have led to significant enhancements of the perceptions of the possibilities of the research.
7. In summary, a better management of the politics of funding, with less distortion and misrepresentation of the scientific realities, could have made a significant difference to outcomes.

The benefits to the project through the collaboration included the following:

1. The motivation for the collaboration was both scientific and commercial, with potential benefits for all participants.
2. While the industrial partner had sensitive interests to protect in respect of the marketplace, and confidentiality was a crucial consideration, there were clearly areas of the collective work which could be published in the open literature without compromising these interests.
3. The primary commercial incentive was the creation of new products on an accelerated timescale, but the raised profile of the company in the relevant literature was also perceived to be of significant value.
4. In this collaboration, several benefits were perceived as key, such as the pooling of resources, the commercial drive and timescale, and the coming together of minds from two worlds. While the objectives of commerce are usually short-term and driven by the demands of the market, this same feature can also be a driving force to energize the more measured pace of academia and accelerate progress.
5. The pooling of resources, of equipment, expertise, and experience, proved to be an accelerator of progress, giving both camps access to facilities which they would not ordinarily have had without the need for significant capital spend.

Further Reading

Nalwa, H.S. (ed.): Ferroelectric Polymers: Chemistry, Physics, and Applications. CRC Press, Boca Raton, FL (1995)

Herbert, J.M., Wand, T.T., Glass, A.M.: The Applications of Ferroelectric Polymers. Chapman & Hall, London (1988)

References

1. Brown, P.H.: Ultrasonic imaging with an electron beam scanned PVdF sensor. Ferroelectrics, **60**, 251–261 (1984). http://www.tandfonline.com/doi/abs/10.1080/00150198408017526
2. Moffatt, M.B., Powers, J.M., McGrath, J.C.: A pc hydrophone. J. Acoust. Soc. Am. **80**, 375–381 (1986)
3. Fukada, E.: History and recent progress in piezoelectric polymers. IEEE Trans. Ultrason. Ferroelectr. Freq. Control **47**, 1277 (2011). http://ieeexplore.ieee.org/document/883516/. doi: 10.1109/58.883516

4. Nix, E.L., Nanayakkara, J., Davies, G.R., Ward, I.M.: Primary and secondary pyroelectricity in highly oriented PVDF. J. Polym. Sci. B **26**, 127–140 (1988). http://onlinelibrary.wiley.com/doi/10.1002/polb.1988.090260107/abstract
5. Capaccio, G., Gibson, A.G., Ward, I.M.: Ultra-High Modulus Polymers (Eds. A.Ciferri, A., Ward, I.M.) Applied Science, Ch. 1. (1979)
6. Capaccio, G., Ward, I.M.: Properties of ultra-high modulus linear polyethylenes. Nature (Phys. Sci.), **243**, 143 (1973). http://www.nature.com/nature-physci/journal/v243/n130/abs/physci243143a0.html
7. Wills, A.J., Capaccio, G., Ward, I.M.: Plastic deformation of polypropylene: Effect of molecular weight on drawing behavior and structural characteristics of ultra-high-modulus products. J. Polym. Sci. **18**, 493 (1980). http://onlinelibrary.wiley.com/doi/10.1002/pol.1980.180180309/full. doi:10.1002/pol.1980.180180309
8. Brew, B., Ward, I.M.: Study of the production of ultra-high modulus polyoxymethylene by tensile drawing at high temperatures. Polymer **19**, 1338–1344 (1978)
9. Nix E.L., Holt, L., McGrath, J.C., Ward, I.M.: Highly drawn PVDF with enhanced mechanical and electrical properties. Ferroelectrics **32**, 103 (1981). http://www.tandfonline.com/doi/abs/10.1080/00150198108238680
10. Humphreys, J., Ward, I.M., Nix, E.L., McGrath, J.C.: A study of the drawing behaviour of PVDF. J. Appl. Polym. Sci. **30**, 4069 (1985). http://onlinelibrary.wiley.com/doi/10.1002/app.1985.070301010/full. doi:10.1002/app.1985.070301010
11. Nix, E.L.: A direct method for measurement of the film-thickness piezoelectric coefficient of PVDF. Ferroelectrics **67**, 125 (1986). http://www.tandfonline.com/doi/abs/10.1080/00150198608245014
12. Humphreys, J., Ward, I.M., McGrath, J.C., Nix, E.L.: The measurement of the piezoelectric coefficients d_{31} and d_{3h} for uniaxially oriented PVDF. Ferroelectrics **67**, 131 (1986). https://www.researchgate.net/publication/241710371_The_measurement_of_the_piezoelectric_coefficients_d31_and_d3h_for_uniaxially_oriented_polyvinylidene_fluoride
13. Nix, E.L., Ward, I.M.: The measurement of the shear piezoelectric coefficients of PVDF. Ferroelectrics **67**, 137 (1986). http://www.tandfonline.com/doi/abs/10.1080/00150198608245016
14. Akindayini, O.O., Nix, E.L., Ward, I.M.: a novel method for the determination of the sheet-thickness compliance of oriented polymers. J. Phys. E: Sci. Instrum. **19**, 911 (1986). http://iopscience.iop.org/article/10.1088/0022-3735/19/11/004
15. Nix, E.L., McGrath, J.C., Holt, L., Ward, I.M., Lewis, E.L.V.: Mechanical and piezoelectric properties of form I vinylidene fluoride polymers for hydrophone applications. Proceedings of 6th IEEE International Symposium on Applications of Ferroelectrics, Lehigh University Bethlehem, PA, pp. 523–526 (1986). http://ieeexplore.ieee.org/document/1538138/?reload=true&arnumber=1538138
16. Humphreys, J., Lewis, E.L.V., Nix, E.L., McGrath, J.C., Ward, I.M.: A study of the mechanical anisotropy of high-draw, low-draw and voided PVDF. J. Polym. Sci. B **26**, 141–158 (1988). http://onlinelibrary.wiley.com/doi/10.1002/polb.1988.090260108/abstract

Chapter 8
Conclusions and Review of the Case Studies

Abstract The current status of academy–industry collaboration is evaluated. Changes in the economic situation have caused knock-on effects in national and state funding of the academy. The benefits and lessons learned from the Case Studies are reviewed and summarized.

Keywords Academy–industry collaboration · Global economic situation · Market-driven environment

8.1 Academy–Industry Collaboration

The academy–industry collaborations in the USA and Europe have been particularly productive especially among leading universities with state-of-the-art research outputs which have had significant potential for commercialization. The European Commission has continued its Framework Programme for Research and Innovation (the current phase is termed H2020) with significant funding opportunities for collaborative projects capable of developing the state of the art in a particular area and able to produce commercializable products which improve the competitive edge of European companies in world markets. Consortia for such collaborative projects are generally a mix of universities, industry, research and development laboratories, and Small and Medium Enterprises (SMEs), with industry generally taking the lead role. The European Research Council acts in parallel to this and has the principal goal of funding high quality research via a competitive bid process and peer evaluation of proposals.

The leading universities in the USA generally have significant internal resources they can devote to developing their relationships with industry. In addition, numerous government agencies provide funds for research and development projects. Further, as noted in Chap. 4, numerous major companies were developed from initial innovative work done in the academy.

Current changes in the global economic situation are resulting in changes in the academy. State funding to institutions in the USA has been reduced. For example,

R. Earnshaw, *Research and Development in the Academy, Creative Industries and Applications*, SpringerBriefs in Computer Science,
DOI 10.1007/978-3-319-54081-8_8

the University of California at Berkeley is currently in a situation where state funding has been reduced to 13% of revenue [1]. This makes it very difficult to fully support the characteristics it has clearly demonstrated in the past as a great public institution. Similar challenges exist across this sector in the USA. There is a trend towards appointing adjunct faculty and other part-time lecturing staff in order to cut costs and also reduce the institution's longer term salary bill. In the USA, an average of 76% of academics are in casual non-permanent posts (with 70% of these being part-time), according to the American Federation of Teachers (AFT), the largest higher education union [2]. Many teach at a number of institutions to generate income—and have to travel between these institutions at their own expense. The AFT calculates that the median pay per course per semester for such staff is around $2700, meaning that an experienced professional teaching three courses a semester might earn only $24,300 a year. The proportion of part-time academic staff is similar in the UK [3, 4], as institutions seek to cut costs.

Although the leading institutions with their internal sources of funding and endowments have only been minimally affected by the economic situation, it has had a major effect on other institutions in their ability to carry forward multiple agendas in teaching, research, industry collaborations, and public engagement. The tendency has been to concentrate on teaching, and publishing research in the most prestigious international journals in order to protect the institution's research reputation and its ranking in league tables. This has resulted in reduced activity in the other areas. The UK government is also seeking to give greater opportunity for private providers to compete for students—thus increasing pressure on existing institutions in the UK. This is likely to divert internal resources to deal with increased competition and a market-driven environment, thus decreasing resources for primary business delivery areas in the academy.

One implication of these developments has resulted in external agencies who are wishing to fund projects to develop industry (and perhaps particularly SMEs for creative industries) also rely on them to get appropriate collaborators together, including the academy. The industrial leader and coordinator assesses the market opportunities and the market needs, and then organizes the consortium to deliver products and services to meet those needs. Some research and development may be needed and the academy is asked to deliver this within a fixed timescale appropriate to the overall project.

8.2 Analyzing the Benefits and the Lessons Learned from the Case Studies

The benefits accruing from the Case Studies and the lessons learned are now reviewed and summarized.

8.2.1 *Shared Virtual and Augmented Environments for Creative Applications*

The academy was closely involved in the development of software to create virtual spaces and enable the user to interact with objects within the space. When there are multiple users interacting with an object, or objects, the environment becomes a shared space. Such users need not necessarily be physically colocated but could access the space via a network link. This offered the opportunity for collaboration on research and development without the need for travel. As it was a 3D space, it was very suitable for application areas where 3D was central. An example is the architectural design of a building, not only to understand the way the building looks within the 3D space available to it, but also how it would feel to a user inside the building after it has been completed. Thus the ability to do virtual walk-throughs within the building gave a good indication of the usability of the building in practice and, where there were perceived deficiencies, these could be rectified at the design stage. The benefits to the user are clear—it enabled a more optimum design to be obtained; it saved money by avoiding the need to change the building after it had been constructed; and it enabled aesthetic issues to be fully addressed (e.g., the external and internal appearance of the building); and also its relationship to neighboring buildings or open spaces. Often such virtual environments needed high-end equipments such as headsets and Caves, though the current trend in entertainment applications is to use TV screens, tablets, or mobile phones, and use the Internet to access the data required, or allow multiple users to access the same space (e.g., as with multiplayer games).

A variety of mobile augmented reality applications enable real and simulated images to be combined. A mobile phone with GPS enables real-time images to be displayed as the user walks around. This is more engaging for the user because it is a dynamic and a real-time experience as the user moves through the real world. Pokemon Go is an example of how mixing modes can be particularly effective as far as the user experience is concerned, and at relatively low cost. This is an example of how augmented reality has become a mass commodity.

It was initially assumed that virtual reality would provide the basis for virtual classrooms for distance learners, and indeed there have been significant achievements in this area. However, they are felt to be too artificial by some learners who prefer more direct real-world interaction than 3D immersion. Thus the combination of real and virtual may be a useful way forward, where the virtual provides 3D assistance to the learner.

8.2.2 Digital Holography as a Creative Medium to Display and Reinterpret Museum Artifacts, Applied to Chinese Porcelain Masterpieces

This project is an excellent example of capitalizing on the synergies between science and art for the creative display and reinterpretation of museum artifacts in order to reveal more about their history; in other words, to combine the objectives of entertainment, cultural awareness, and education. The redefinition, recreation, reconstruction, and representation was successfully applied to the art works from the archaeological excavation of the site. This site involved the largest quantity of a major Chinese cultural artifact, Yuan blue-and-white porcelain. The recreation of the scene of the discovery of the porcelain was successfully field-tested in a major exhibition in Beijing.

The project illustrates the benefits of using technology to enable the production of fuller information on the history of the artifacts and their discovery; to use synthetic holograms as a creative art form; and to provide larger screen displays to enable viewers to see more of the detail. It was believed that ordinary 2D photographs were rapidly becoming unattractive to museum visitors as they now expect something much more dynamic and state of the art, given what is now possible with off-the-shelf technology such as 3D television and mobile phones in the home environment.

One downside with holographic representation is that the current equipment is expensive and requires specialist skills to operate. Thus for wider use, lower cost facilities are needed which are easy to use. Over time it is possible that commoditization may result in the lowering of costs and greater ease of use. Innovation should eventually lead to better facilities via evolution and developmental processes. Often a “killer application” can provide incentives and motivation to developers to get a suitable product to market in the shortest possible time, in order to capitalize on the potential market opportunities.

8.2.3 Improving the Physical Properties of Materials by Collaboration Between Industry and the Academy

This Case Study illustrates a more classical approach to collaboration where the academy and industry joined together in order to further the research and development needed to improve the physical properties of materials. This highlighted the difficulties (noted in earlier chapters) of ensuring that most of the primary motivations of each partner in the collaboration could be met. Industry requires the new materials in the shortest possible time while keeping the processes involved confidential in order to maintain an edge on the commercial competition. At the same time, the academy’s researchers need to be able to publish research papers in order to maintain their position within the academy. Clearly there is a tension between these two objectives and it needed careful discussion and agreement of what could be published and what could not. However, the collaboration had the benefit of ensuring that scientific research and investigation was directed at an area that was potentially commercializable, rather than simply generating knowledge for its own sake. This was clearly very useful for both parties. Further, the industrial partner subsequently realized the benefits brought about by the publications raising the profile of the work done. In addition, it was clear that the collaboration accelerated progress on the work by the combination of complementary resources, skills, and expertise, and also enabled the work to be done on a more economic basis than if each partner had attempted to do the work on their own.

8.3 Further Case Studies

Further case studies are available online [5–14].

Further Reading

Douglass, J.A.: The New Flagship University: Changing the Paradigm from Global Ranking to National Relevancy (International and Development Education), p. 240. Palgrave Macmillan, London (2016)

References

1. Gaskell, S., Collette, A.: The benefits of engagement. Times Higher Education, pp. 37–39, 8 Dec 2016. https://www.timeshighereducation.com/features/the-benefits-of-engagement
2. http://www.academica.ca/blog/part-time-faculty-what-we-know-and-what-we-dont, http://www.chronicle.com/blogs/conversation/2015/05/12/an-adjuncts-farewell/, https://www.aaup.org/issues/contingency/background-facts
3. Casual contracts are ruining universities for staff and students. The Guardian, 12 Feb 2016. https://www.theguardian.com/higher-education-network/2016/feb/12/casual-contracts-are-ruining- universities-for-staff-and-students
4. https://www.ucu.org.uk/article/8154/Precarious-contracts-in-HE—institution-snapshot, https://www.theguardian.com/commentisfree/2016/nov/17/universities-casual-contracts-casualised-work-profit-academia-staff-students, https://www.theguardian.com/uk-news/2016/nov/16/universities-accused-of-importing-sports-direct-model-for-lecturers-pay
5. Miles, I., Green, L.: Hidden innovation in the creative industries. Research Report, p. 84, Nesta, 2008. https://www.nesta.org.uk/sites/default/files/hidden_innovation_creative_industries_report.pdf
6. Arts and culture case studies. http://www.thecreativeindustries.co.uk/industries/arts-culture/arts-culture-case-studies
7. Case study in emerging industries. An analysis of industry-specific framework conditions for the development of world-class clusters in *creative industries*. http://www.emergingindustries.eu/framework-conditions/creative-industries.aspx

8. Ten inspiring case studies about culture and creative industries. https://www.culture-partnership.eu/en/article/10-inspiring-case-studies
9. Bakker, G.: Supporting the development and success of the creative industries. London School of Ecomomics. http://www.lse.ac.uk/researchAndExpertise/researchImpact/caseStudies/bakker-supporting-development-and-success-of-creative-industries.aspx, http://www.lse.ac.uk/research And Expertise/researchImpact/PDFs/Bakker.pdf
10. Games. http://www.thecreativeindustries.co.uk/industries/games
11. Digital arts and media—we want to find new ways to help our creative industries thrive. http://www.nesta.org.uk/areas-work/digital-arts-and-media?gclid=CMm2p62Z7dACFUa4GwodEO4Jkg
12. Searle, N.: Changing business models in the creative industries: the cases of Television, Computer Games and Music. UK government (2011). https://www.gov.uk/government/publications/changing-business-models-in-the-creative-industries, https://www.gov.uk/government/ uploads/system/uploads/attachment_data/file/310299/ipresearch-creativeind-sum-201110.pdf, https://www.gov.uk/government/uploads/system/uploads/attachment_data/file/310293/ipresearch-creativeind-full-201110.pdf
13. Creative Industries—Business & Employment in the Arts: Measuring the Scope of the Nation's Arts-Related Industries. http://www.americansforthearts.org/by-program/reports-and-data/research-studies-publications/creative-industries
14. Creative Industries and the European Union. http://www.cbi.org.uk/insight-and-analysis/creative-industries-and-the-eu/

MIX
Papier aus verantwortungsvollen Quellen
Paper from responsible sources
FSC® C105338

If you have any concerns about our products,
you can contact us on
ProductSafety@springernature.com

In case Publisher is established outside the EU,
the EU authorized representative is:
Springer Nature Customer Service Center GmbH
Europaplatz 3, 69115 Heidelberg, Germany

Printed by Libri Plureos GmbH
in Hamburg, Germany